T0103008

# Guests of
# Itlldo Place
# Bed and Breakfast

## A Year's Diary of Our Guests

### DANA WOOD-BOISSONNEAULT

Order this book online at www.trafford.com
or email orders@trafford.com

Most Trafford titles are also available at major online book retailers.

© Copyright 2010 Dana Wood-Boissonneault.
All rights reserved. No part of this publication may be reproduced, stored in a retrieval system, or
transmitted, in any form or by any means, electronic, mechanical, photocopying, recording, or
otherwise, without the written prior permission of the author.

Printed in Victoria, BC, Canada.

ISBN: 978-1-4269-2314-2

*Our mission is to efficiently provide the world's finest, most comprehensive book publishing
service, enabling every author to experience success. To find out how to publish your book, your
way, and have it available worldwide, visit us online at www.trafford.com*

*Trafford rev. 4/01/2010*

www.trafford.com

**North America & international**
toll-free: 1 888 232 4444 (USA & Canada)
phone: 250 383 6864 ♦ fax: 812 355 4082

☺

For
Roger and Leslie
Thank you for
All your work at
Itlldo Place B&B!

# Itlldo Place Bed and Breakfast

# Donnelly, Alberta, Canada

What would it be like to have a bed and breakfast? What kind of guests would we get? Would it be a good idea to have one in Donnelly, a village in northern Alberta of less than 300 people? Roger, a local farmer, our preteen daughter Leslie, and myself Dana, were going to find out! None of us had stayed at a bed and breakfast before, people in the area were not familiar with the B&B sign on our building, yet we felt confident that the idea would succeed! Both of our families thought that we were crazy to take on such a task! We were living a comfortable life, in a normal house, that was just about paid off. Why move, take on such an enormous workload and uncertainty, with huge financial costs? I knew that I could always count on the income from my teaching job to keep us afloat however, and the people that we met were more than rewarding enough. Where else could you meet and learn about so many people, without even leaving your own home?

# January

## Sunday, January 1

No guests were here. It was the start of a brand new year. Who would be coming in through our door this year? Would they come because of business or for holidays? Would they be from Canada, the United States or Europe? Would they like our unique, renovated restaurant and bar, bed and breakfast? Only time would tell if the previous years of experience, would enable us to have a smooth running, day-to-day operation of our business.

## Friday, January 6

☻ The doorbell rang at 8:05 p.m. There standing in the moonlight, with snow softly falling down, was Barb from Manning. Barb had dark, curly hair, was 30ish and anxious to check out the place. Her eyes lit up when we entered the 4 000 sq. foot main floor. The rope lights around the counters, the pillars and the exercise area were all on. A soft glow of light filtered down from the upper floor. She was delighted and booked two rooms; the double and the bunk bed rooms. Her two sons were playing hockey in McLennan. They came back around 10:15 p.m. The code for the door beeped away, the door opened and squeals of delight were emitted as the boys checked out the four-in-one play area. The pool table was their favorite. They also played ringette on the dance floor, and plunked away on the keyboards. They were all tucked in by 11:10 p.m.

## Saturday, January 7

Barb appreciated the free breakfast of waffles, toast, and fruit. She came back with two of her girlfriends to show them the place in the afternoon, along with a hockey dad. Pete had one boy. Pete said that they would come next weekend and travel to Valleyview for the hockey tournament. He said that he would phone some other people to see if they would book up the rest of the rooms.

## Monday, January 9

☻ 7:30 p.m. The Busy Bee Motel in McLennan was wondering if we had any rooms available for tonight. Sandra was the only woman, traveling with five men. They arrived in an older van. Their job was to sell cleaning products to oil rig workers and people in the towns. Sandra went to the washroom while Roy and Burt talked to my husband Roger. Topics ranged from farming to hockey. Roy proudly stated that he could solve our Rubric's cube. He said that you have to solve one side and then keep on going, twisting each side in turn. Burt enjoyed playing with the remote-controlled helicopter. Steve, with grey hair, found a place on one of the couches and fell asleep in front of the big screen television. He had strummed away on the guitar for half an hour. They had been up since 6:00 a.m. Greg and Tim played a game of cards. The game stopped whenever Tim had to go outside for a smoke. Tim's favorite pun was, "A hole has been found in the nudist camp wall. The police are looking into it!" They were a friendly lot! The last two went to bed at midnight. They'll only grab a cup of coffee in the morning.

## Tuesday, January 10

☺ 7:55 a.m. Pete booked two rooms for the weekend coming up. There is a hockey tournament in Valleyview. Pete and his son will take up the other room.

The doorbell chimed away its post Christmas greeting at 4:25 p.m. A couple in their 60s, were smiling sadly at us. The fellow, Victor, had been driving since yesterday. They had come from Vernon, British Columbia, for his uncle's funeral. Their last night's sleep wasn't very good. A fellow must have fallen asleep watching television in the adjacent hotel room. Their bed was on the other side of the television and they didn't get much sleep. His wife, Cecile, reminisced about Uncle Pierre who had died at the age of 94. He had had a hard life, and ended up slowly losing his memory due to Alzheimer's disease. He had spent the last years of his life deaf in a nursing home, in adult diapers, being fed mashed up food, and then ended up getting gangrene in his foot. It was a blessing in a way that he died. He was married for 68 years. Victor overheard this joke: A small boy swallowed some coins and was taken to a hospital. His grandmother telephoned to ask how he was and a nurse said, "No change yet!" They will be leaving 'early' in the morning, at 8:00 a.m. Victor is one of the pallbearers and doesn't want to be late.

3

# Wednesday, January 11

☺ 8:10 a.m. A hockey team from Spirit River was trying to book all of the rooms for the weekend. We had to turn them down, but we did give them numbers of other bed and breakfast operators in the area.

● 6:55 p.m., the Busy Bee Motel gave us the phone number for more potential customers. I phoned the booking lady for the oil rig crew, but because we were already booked up for the weekend with the hockey gang, and they wanted to stay in one place for a whole week, they decided not to stay with us.

Just like her e-mail booking stated, Jessica arrived after supper. It was her third visit with us. The first time, she came with her husband Philip. They liked it so much that they stayed for five days! Philip thought of the catchy slogan "Room to Roam" for us. We needed the slogan for the Travel Alberta website that we had registered with. For some reason the code for the keyless-entry door did not work, so she rang the doorbell. Looking splendid in her new pink coat from Christmas, she quickly brought in her books. She goes to schools in the area to help French-learning students how to speak properly. I had a bundle of French booklets that I no longer needed on the table in her room waiting for her. She offered to pay for them, but I declined her offer. Her two sons were off to exotic lands for six months. One on a mission in Mexico, the other one was around the Panama Canal area. They both wanted financial help from their parents of course! Jessica asked about the puppies that had been just born during her last visit. They had all been sold except for the first-born puppy that my daughter Leslie had fallen in love with. She also asked to see pictures of Leslie's

4

cruise with her grandmother, to the Hawaiian Islands. Jessica liked to stay in her room and read. I was glad that the three oil rig workers from Newfoundland changed their minds about staying with us for the night.

## Thursday, January 12

We got two phone calls tonight, half and hour apart, canceling out for this weekend. That was disheartening, because we had turned down a hockey team just yesterday morning, for the weekend, and an oil rig crew who wanted to stay a whole week. "Sorry" hardly seemed fair.

The Busy Bee Motel phoned again at 5:35 p.m., seeing if we had any rooms available for tonight. Kim, a 46 year old man came to our door 15 minutes later. He and Roger got along really well. They talked and laughed most of the evening away, especially when Kim said, "I wondered why the baseball kept getting bigger. Then it hit me!" Kim sells vehicle equipment parts. He is in the area several times a year. Perhaps he too will become one of our regulars.

## Friday, January 13

☻ 4:40 p.m. Sue, a saleslady, wanted to book an appointment for us to put our bed and breakfast in her oilfield telephone directory. She was very impressed at how immaculate the outside looked with all of the rock work, and was equally amazed at the inside. She ended up enrolling in the Mannatech health company that we had a display on, and promised to come back and buy a whole bunch of Usborne books from our great selection. After admiring our sport stacking display, she said that she had heard about sport stacking. It is an officially recognized sport of stacking cups. She tried doing the 3 stack and the 6 stack. She requested a whole bunch of business cards to give to the executives. She was quite certain that she would be back, and was looking forward to listening to more of Roger's music that he composes. Sue was intrigued with the name of this place. After I explained that after looking extensively for a new home, my great auntie in England finally said, "It'll do" to her husband. It has become a family tradition to name our homes with the "It will do" expression. Sue thought that the expression was from the sheep-herding fellows who say "It'll do" when the dogs have completed their job well. I had never heard of that before!

## Saturday, January 14

☻ 2:00 p.m. Biff called from Athabaska, to say that he wouldn't be able to stop by for a visit. He and his wife stayed with us two years ago, while attending his uncle's funeral. His uncle died in an automobile accident on the highway. Biff sells Zambonis and was planning on visiting with us for awhile, but with the sun setting at 4:40 p.m. at this time of year, his wife thought that it would be best for him to carry on home to Hussar. Biff will come in the spring, to help us install the fountain in the pond that he is loaning us.

## Sunday, January 15

☻ 6:30 p.m. Jake and Simon arrived from Prince Edward Island. They were in the area to finish up completing the new hockey arena. They were very quiet men who worked all day, then went to their rooms all tuckered out. Their secretary said that they would be here for one week.

## Monday, January 16

I got an interesting e-mail from Wayne in Edmonton. Wayne stayed with us for two nights, pretty well a year ago. He was called to fix the organ in Donnelly's church. It was quite the tune-up, with a lot of the parts spread on the church's floor. His adorable little Yorkie didn't seem to mind the long hours. Wayne was quite the photographer, and quite often sent me these fantastic nature pictures. His latest was a picture of a girl and what seemed to be a real snow ghost. He later explained that she had pressed her face into some freshly fallen snow and then he had taken the picture! Could have fooled me!

## Tuesday, January 17

Some fire trucks racing by reminded me of one of our guests that we had during our first year of operation. Bob, from Farmington New Mexico, was making his way back to the United States, having traveled all the way up to the Northwest Territories on a canoe trip with some buddies. He was one of the firefighters who was called to put out the Pentagon fire during the 9/11 crisis. He told us in an emotional voice about how hard that day was. For a grown man to have tears in his eyes recollecting the horrors, that will probably be with him for the rest of his life, was very moving. Bob gave us big hugs and had his picture taken with us by our big smiley-face B&B sign, which faces highway #2.

## *Wednesday, January 18*

☻ 5:05 p.m. James' cell phone connection kept on breaking off, so he called again. He could hear me talking, but I couldn't hear him. He was aware of the dangers of driving using cell phones, but not that after two minutes of use, the blood-brain barrier in our brains allow proteins and poisons in. James stayed with us in October for two nights, but because Telus doesn't provide high-speed internet access to Donnelly yet, he decided to stay in Peace River to do his oil-related business. Most of the hotels there have high-speed internet. James will be staying with us again for two nights. He has his own extension cord for his truck. It was going to go down to minus 22 during the night. Roger and James gave each other a friendly greeting before they started talking about playing hockey and the upcoming tournament. James quite often plays some games if he is in the area. He didn't have his equipment this trip, because he was flying back to his hometown of Calgary. He had some business appointments in Falher tomorrow. The oil companies give James a maximum amount of dollars that he can go up to, to buy land for the rigs. It is up to James to get the land from the farmers, for as little as possible. James nodded his head as he admired the lit-up miniature village street that was put up after Christmas. It was on a long shelf, taking up the whole length of the three bed and breakfast rooms. He was happy to be back.

# Thursday, January 19

James said that his bed was so comfortable that he didn't want to get up in the morning! He was off to Falher, Nampa, and Peace River today. He managed to squeeze in some time to chat with the Donnelly Capital hockey players after their game at the Guy-Donnelly Sportex, which finished at 11 p.m. Roger had a surprise for him- he had taped the Flames and Canadians hockey game. Three other fellows came over to watch the Flame's victory with a close 3-2 score. They munched on Cheese Pleesers, and Nacho Cheese flavoured tortilla chips. One thirty in the morning came quickly!

# Sunday, January 22

☻ 2:20 p.m. Catherine, the band teacher from the local junior high/high school, is having a conductor come in on the first weekend in February for her students. She wanted to know if we had room for him. He should have a good time here with all of our instruments that he could play!

# Monday, January 23

Surprise, surprise! Guess who came back in the queen room again for three more nights? James! Roger was up on a chair going to replace a sensor light when he came in. Good timing too, because James said not to change it! He had unscrewed it last time, because it kept on going on! It must have been the wind that night bringing in a Chinook. Sometimes the weather does strange things to the sensor lights, especially lightning storms. He thoughtfully left his one suitcase that he had rolled through the snow, to drip in the boot room. James requested a short extension cord so that he could plug in his computer and printer at the same time. First things first though, he watched hockey on the television before getting down to work!

## Tuesday, January 24

James and I exchanged good wishes for the day as he went out to his already started white truck. He came back at 5:30 p.m. and then left again for a meeting at 7:00 p.m. in Falher. He sure works long days. Good thing there was hockey to watch on the TV to relax to!

## Wednesday, January 25

James said that he wouldn't be back until late, but we were not expecting him to be back at 2:10 in the morning. He was officially the latest guest ever to come in of over 200 people! He had to drive all the way to Grande Cache to pick up a radio that he needed to go out in the bush with and then drive the three hours again to return it. Seven hours later, he had to head back to Calgary.

☺

## Thursday, January 26

☻ 6:10 p.m. Danée arrived radiating with so much happiness at finding plenty of historical information, from the local genealogical library! She was interested in the Métis research.

## Friday, January 27

Danée was planning on staying only one night, but decided to stay one more night before heading back to Fort St. John. She said that she would recommend the library and our place to her fellow researchers!

## Saturday, January 28

☺ 1:30 a.m. Yes, that was the arrival time of Aden and Melanie. We had given up on them! They had left Edmonton later then they should of, because they did not want to miss a party that was going on at a Greek restaurant. The skating instructors slept in until noon, then were off to evaluate skating at the local arena.

## Sunday, January 29

Four swinging 70s seniors came for the night. Their auntie had passed away at the age of 94, so they were in for her funeral. They were a lively bunch who enjoyed Roger's piano recital, danced a bit on the dance floor, and took lots of digital pictures! Roland got everyone laughing with his joke about the butcher who backed into a meat grinder and got a little behind in his work!

# February

## Wednesday, February 1

☻ Carla phoned at 5:35 p.m. to book up one room for her family. Her 14 year old boy would be playing hockey in Donnelly and McLennan in two weeks. She had taken note of our place the last time that she had passed by Donnelly. She only wanted one room, even though it would work out to only $5 more to put her son in the bunk bed room, instead of a sleeping bag. Who knows, she might change her mind when she gets here.

## Thursday, February 2

James was back again. His name is getting pretty well known around here! He might be spending four to five days with us! He expertly punched in the code for the door and gave a booming greeting to Roger. James laid his hockey stuff out on the dance floor. He had come prepared to play hockey this time, and to help out during the hockey tournament that Roger puts on every year. What a nice fellow! James did some phone calls, before he headed out for awhile, but not before telling Roger that if he heard some sounds coming from his room, that it would only be his printer working.

13

# Friday, February 3

☻ Harold, the conductor, arrived at 6:45 p.m., but he didn't want to come in until Catherine, the local band teacher, showed up at 7:00 p.m. He waited patiently in his truck. Catherine was eager to have a tour of the place. She had been in the place when it was a bar, but not since then. She was impressed with all of the things to do. About 190 students from Donnelly, High Prairie, Whitecourt and Slave Lake would be in Donnelly for the weekend, attending workshops from various musicians. The students are sleeping in the classrooms with chaperones. It is the seventh year that a band bash would be going on. Catherine and Harold headed out for a tour of the school in Donnelly, and to grab a bite to eat. It was going to be a long weekend for both of them! Harold came back at 9:45 p.m. He was so tuned into humming his music scores, that he never even noticed me checking up on the pellet stove. He was getting ready for a student marching band exercise. Harold was quite amazed at the restaurant in Falher. While eating his steak, he heard French, broken English, and even a booming Newfoundlander's voice. Everyone was very friendly. Harold has been taking band students all over the world now for over thirty years. He recollected that back then, most of the students from Grande Prairie hadn't even been to Edmonton, let alone on a plane. He has noticed a big difference in security, with the United States being the most prudent. Passports are essential now.

☺

# Saturday, February 4

James is a tired but happy fellow, coming back at 2:00 a.m. with a MVP medallion. He scored two goals and three assists in the hockey game. He phoned his wife at 5:20 p.m. to tell her that he now had two most valuable player medallions. He was pleased as punch! James had a quick shower and then went off to get supper and to work.

Harold came back for five minutes at 5:35 p.m., before returning to the school for more sessions. Everyone was pleased with the great weather that we had been having.

# Sunday, February 5

The Cocktail Banana hockey team that James played with, did not win the tournament. He had fun trying anyway. James did win $100 on a Super Bowl bet. It was the Steelers against the Seahawks. The Steelers won 21 to 10. Harold had three hours more of instruction to do before heading back to Grande Prairie.

# Monday, February 6

☺ James took off at 9:00 a.m. and did not return until 10:20 p.m. He did a lot of catching up on work since he took most of the weekend off to play hockey. I got an interesting e-mail reservation from Sylvie. She works for the Alberta government and wants to spend four nights with us in May with her two pets. She didn't even know where we were located! I wonder how she found out about us! I e-mailed her back a confirmation.

## Tuesday, February 7

☺ James paid up and left at 9:00 a.m., his usual time. This will be the last that we see of him until next year's tournament, because he has accepted a higher paying desk job as a supervisor. I will e-mail him our congratulations!

## Wednesday, February 8

☻ 6:15 p.m. The door chime went. It was Marc, a senior citizen whose trailer pipes had frozen, and needed a place to stay until the weather warmed up! He was happy to go in the bunk bed room, however we needed to take the top bunk out and put it on the dance floor, so that he could get in and out of bed easier. He knitted by the pellet stove which was good for his arthritis. He also liked to play card games like Bridge, with Roger. He had safety in mind when he quipped, "Don't join dangerous cults: Practice safe sects!"

## Friday, February 10

☻ Da Skates hockey team from Grande Cache stayed one night. The eight fellows wasted no time in getting a poker game started! They were good sports when they lost! They either watched the others play or watched hockey on the television. Four got to sleep in the rooms and four got comfortable on foamies with their sleeping bags. Doug the coach said that they would definitely be back next year for a rematch!

## Saturday, February 11

☻Carla, her husband and son arrived around 8:00 p.m. to say that they were here and that they were going to get some supper. They came back an hour later. Driving all the way from High Level and watching her son play hockey in Donnelly, all played a toll on Carla. She was soon fast asleep on the couch, as her family watched TV. They all went to bed at the same time. Her son ended up in the bunk bed room for the same price as a sleeping bag.

## Sunday, February 12

☺Carla's son had a game in McLennan at 10:00 a.m. After the game, they were off to Edmonton to get on a jet to fly to Mexico for a ten day vacation. Talk about zooming about!

## Monday, February 13

James just couldn't stay away from our place! He had some loose ends to finish up, before his new job could start. His familiar code to unlock the door was punched in at 6:05 p.m. He unloaded his work equipment then headed out for supper. He was relaxing by the TV with some pop by 8:45 p.m. He had a close call with a mule deer on the road. Good thing the mule deer decided to hurry across the road and her buddies decided to stay where they were. An accident with a deer can cost thousands of dollars in repair. There are around 12 000 crashes a year on Alberta roads involving animals. The most likely time to hit one is in November when it is mating season.

## Tuesday, February 14

☺James was gone for a day of work at 7:35 a.m. He phoned at 8:55 p.m. to say that he had to meet with a client at the hockey arena in Peace River. The fellow had to watch his son play hockey and had time to do business there. James won't be back until around 11:00 p.m. He'll leave the money for us on the guestbook. He signed our book too. It is interesting to read the comments in there.

☺

# Some Guestbook comments:

- Absolutely lovely home - beautiful!

- Funky and artsy.

- I love listening to your frogs.

- Wow, what fun! Unbelievable!

- Nice & comfy.

- We enjoyed your creativity & your energy!

- Nice to meet you! Thanks so much.

- The Most Cleanest Bathroom Ever, 5 Stars *****.

- I love the way your place stimulates the imagination.

- Awesome place. Keep it up!

- Hang around for the piano concert - it's worth the wait!!

- It's been great to get to know you. God bless!

- ABSOLUTELY AMAZING!!

- Very relaxing and spacious.

- Love it here. Doing a great job! Hope to be back soon.

- Thanks for a great stay! Super!

- Thanks for the great hospitality. Nice talking to you.

- Thank you for the excellent stay. Wonderful visit!

- Merci pour tout. Un endroit vraiment accueillant.

- Thanks a million. Nice place.

- Thanks for your hospitality.

- I really like your bright colors!! Especially the purple!! Thanks for making our anniversary room special w/the flower petals & table items.

- Thank you for having us & showing us around your lovely home.

- Thank you is not enough for the warm welcome and best accommodation you've given us!

- Such nice gestures will be remembered and treasured by us forever!

☺

## Wednesday, February 15

☺ The phone rang at 9:45 a.m. It was Cecile, calling all the way from Quebec! Her family is moving to Falher at the end of the month, and the local insurance lady recommended us to her. They will stay with their little dog for two nights, while they make arrangements for a permanent place. I wonder if we will be speaking more French than English that weekend!

## Friday, February 17

● 11:30 p.m. A hockey team from Grande Prairie started to arrive. They had a tournament to play in and would be leaving on Sunday. They were very much in a party mood.

## Saturday, February 18

☺ 7:00 a.m. The fellows noisily started to get ready for their first game. They were in and out throughout the day. They left empty glasses and beer cans all over the place. I was glad when they finally left to go party elsewhere!

## Sunday, February 19

The lot of them did not get back until seven in the morning! Our dogs started to bark with all the loud noises going on. This woke me up and I wretched my back out of place. What a bunch of inconsiderate people. One was so drunk that he spilt beer on my brand-new couch. They never woke up until

1:15 p.m. and it was then that they realized that they had left their keys in their truck. It cost them $45.00 plus G.S.T. to get a locksmith to open it. They are never welcome back! It took many hours to clean up after that lot. Thank goodness most people are not like that. I made up some bed and breakfast rules that I put in each room because of that lot.

# Itlldo Place B&B Rules

Welcome to our bed and breakfast, our home! If you would like to stay with us, we ask that you follow these rules.

## ARRIVAL

- Guests are allowed to park on the bricks.

- Outdoor footwear needs to be removed and placed on the racks.

- Outside doors need to be locked at all times, unless you are just going out for a few minutes and will be coming right back.

## LIGHTS AND APPLIANCES

- Lights need to be turned off, when you are not in the room.

- Rope lights will be on during the evening and throughout the night.

- TV should be at a reasonable volume and turned off when you leave.

- Coffee pot and other kitchen appliances need to be turned off after use.

## CLEANING

- Vacuuming and dusting are done on a weekly basis.

- If guests are present, vacuuming, cleaning the kitchen area, and the bathrooms are done after each visit.

- Guests who pay to have breakfast, leave their dishes for us to clean. This is done upstairs.

- Guests who bring their own food are responsible to clean their own dishes.

- Dishes are sanitized as needed in the upstairs dishwasher.

- Bottles and cans go in the white container by the kitchen garbage.

- Newspapers are to be put in the basket by the kitchen garbage.

- Wrappers and other garbage are not to be left around our place. Garbage containers are located in each room, each bathroom, in the kitchen and by the front door.

## WASHROOMS

- Towels will be washed at the end of your visit or after a week, whichever comes first. Please use the towel racks to hang up your towel to dry.

- Toilets and urinals need to be flushed.

- Zest soap products are not to be used in the showers.

☺

## ROOMS

- During the summer, blinds and drapes should be closed to keep the heat out, and your door left open if you want a cooler room.

- During the fall, winter and early spring, all blinds need to be opened during the day to allow for solar heating.

- Hangars in the wardrobes are to be left in the wardrobe.

- Guests are to sleep in between the sheets, not on the blankets.

- Pillows with shams on them are for decorative purposes only. Extra pillows to sleep with are located in the wardrobes.

- We will only go in your room to clean it after your visit, or to change your sheets after a week's visit.

## EXERCISE EQUIPMENT

- Use care when using the exercise equipment.

- Use the orange cord to plug in the elliptical machine, before getting on it.

- Guests taking outdoor equipment to be used outside, must bring the balls etc. back in after using it.

## CHILDREN

- Children need to be supervised at all times, especially by the dugout.

- If your child breaks something, you need to pay for it.

- If your child makes a mess, you need to clean it up.

- All toys and games need to be put away after each use.

- Young children should not be using the exercise equipment.

- Children should not be playing the piano, nor keyboards.

- Toddlers need to be within reaching distance when they are awake.

- Children are not to rotate the four-in-one (hockey, air hockey, pool and foosball)

- Children need to be supervised when using the paint and drawing area. Paper is located in the golden trunk by the ramp going to the dance floor.

## PETS

- We have dogs, cats, birds and fish. The fish are the only ones accessible to guests.

- Your pets are welcome to stay if they stay off of the beds and furniture.

- All paws need to be cleaned before entering.

- Any messes need to be picked up by the owner.

- Accidents on the carpet will be charged $10.

## MUSICAL INSTRUMENTS

- The piano and keyboards are off limits unless you know how to play them.

- Keyboards need to be turned off when you are done.

- Drinks and food are not allowed on or near the piano and keyboards.

## THINGS TO BUY

- Usborne books need to be bought before being read. Receipts are located on the table by the kitchen. As a special rate to our guests, GST and shipping will be paid by us. Other books and magazines are free for you to read.

- Mannatech health products are available by enrolling with the company which Dana can do for you. You then buy the products over the phone or on the computer.

- Sportstacking sets are available for $50. This includes the cups, DVD, written instructions, a bag for the cups, timer, mat and bag for the mat and timer.

- Long distance rates from 6pm to 8am are 10cents/minute, otherwise it is 30cents/minute.

- Paying for your room is by cash or cheque, payable to Dana Wood-Boissonneault.

## GUESTS

- Smoking is allowed outside only. Containers are by each door.

- Guests are not allowed upstairs.

- Quiet time starts at 10pm to 7am.

- Be considerate of people who are sleeping if you arrive late. Close the doors quietly and talk quietly.

- Please ring the green bell by the door if you need to get our attention, or write us a note.

- Please double check that you have all of your belongings before leaving.

- Unregistered guests who are visiting for a bit and are not staying with us, must follow all of the above rules.

- People who do not follow our rules might be asked to leave.

BE RESPONSIBLE, SHOW RESPECT AND BE HONEST.

Dana, Roger and Leslie Boissonneault

# Monday, February 20

☻ 6:15 p.m. Emma, Matthew and Tyler arrived from Edmonton. They had a good drive down with no snow problems. The food scientists were eager to solve the problem of having honey not solidifying in a plastic bag, after a few months. They were going to test if it was the air, water content, or temperature that may be the factor. They were buzzing with ideas over breakfast!

# Tuesday, February 21

Wayne, the organ repair fellow was in Toronto. He sent me a cute e-mail. Here it is! CAT IN THE HAT ON AGING. I cannot see. I cannot pee. I cannot chew. I cannot screw.

Oh my god, what can I do? My memory shrinks. My hearing stinks. No sense of smell. I look like hell. My mood is bad-can you tell? My body's drooping. Have trouble pooping. The Golden Years have come at last. The Golden Years can kiss my ass!

## *Wednesday, February 22*

☻ The phone rang at 3:05 p.m. It was Charles and Sam from Wainwright, looking for some rooms for tonight. Charles had been in the area before and they wanted to check our place out this trip. They worked for the oilfield, checking in on the guys to make sure that they were doing things safely, and if there were any concerns, that they would help to mediate. Charles' wife was a grade two teacher for seventeen years. Sam has teachers in his family too. Charles knew about the local honey producer Heinz. He was interested in knowing that Heinz has a new honey product out in his Guy factory. Charles had actually gone salmon fishing with Heinz a couple of years back. He recounted how Heinz was so proud of himself for catching the biggest salmon. Every time a big catch came in, Heinz would go and check it out to make sure that he was still the trophy winner. Charles' brother had caught a bigger salmon, but he didn't want to tell Heinz until the ceremony. Boy was Heinz disappointed. He apparently had quite the expression on his face! Sam was interested in the Mannatech miracle stories. He also wanted to make sure that the alarm clocks worked, as he had to get up at 6 a.m.

☺

## Friday, February 24

Cecile and her family from Quebec never showed up. Oh well, maybe tomorrow night.

☻ 10:30 p.m. Kam, his wife and five kids, arrived from Edmonton. We had set up a tent on the dance floor for the kids. They thought that it was pretty cool to be tenting inside in the winter! Kam's oldest son was autistic and had to thoroughly explore our place before settling in for the night.

## Saturday, February 25

No word from Cecile, not even a phone call.

## Sunday, February 26

Lina phoned, asking if Cecile had arrived. Lina is the owner of the rental property that Cecile was supposed to be renting. Cecile never even had the courtesy to phone Lina about not coming.

## Monday, February 27

☻ The doorbell rang out its Beethoven First Symphony tune after one o'clock. It was Mrs. Drouin. She was here to check out the place for her visiting elderly friend Mrs. Blanchette. Mrs. Blanchette might come next week.

# Tuesday, February 28

☻The phone rang at 12:20 p.m. It was a hockey team from Lacombe, looking for a place for 48 people for the upcoming provincial tournament in March. We have room for 22 people, putting most on foamies and sleeping bags. Sue will get back to us.

# March

## Wednesday, March 1

Brianna phoned all the way from Calgary, inquiring if this was the Itlldo Place Hotel. I was going to say that it was a bed and breakfast but decided to agree with the hotel word. After all, the place is big enough to be a hotel! Her sister had recommended us, saying that we were an excellent place to stay at. Can't go wrong with word of mouth advertising! It turned out that her sister was Makayla. Makayla used to be married to one of Roger's cousins! Brianna and her husband Justin booked up for a whole week, after finding out our weekly rate. Their two girls might come with sleeping bags too. There is a big 75th anniversary reunion in Guy, during the first weekend in July. Guy is a hop and a skip south of Donnelly.

## Thursday, March 2

It was too bad that David Bouchard, a literacy/advocate for children, had a room booked up already in High Prairie. David is a 53 year old Métis dyslexic speaker who did not read a full book until he was 27 years old. He was traveling around the world spreading the message to parents to turn off the technology in their homes and to give the gift of reading to their children. For parents who scoffed at buying twenty dollar books, he asked them to think about how much they spend on cell phones, internet, computer games, cable, or satellite costs for television every month. He said that just as babies develop at different times, so does their ability to learn how to read, and to never give up on them. So many doors are closed to people who do not know how to read in our society. If you are interested in buying some of his books, you can go to his awesome website at www.DavidBouchard.com. He also had some links to buy aboriginal flutes. The C pentatonic elderberry flute that he had played during his presentation in Falher, had an enchanting sound.

## Friday, March 3

Sue and Debra phoned to book rooms for their families for the upcoming hockey tournament in McLennan. They would be staying Thursday, Friday and Saturday night. They got our name from the Busy Bee Motel in McLennan.

☻ 9:45 p.m. Annabelle and Eric were in town to evaluate figure skaters tomorrow. They had quite the animated discussion on how the level of expertise has fallen. The standards are still there to be met, but today's youth are not reaching those levels. The parents get upset with the evaluators and say that they are too tough on their kids. Annabelle thinks that she will retire soon and Eric is worried that not enough younger people are working their way to become evaluators, so pretty soon the parents will have more to complain about!

☺

## Saturday, March 4

☻ Lucienne phoned at 8:05 p.m. to make a reservation for the last weekend in the month, for her mother's birthday. She was from Falher, but resides in Red Deer now, so she knew where we were located.

## Sunday, March 5

☺ 8:10 p.m. Tina arrived without any winter coat or boots. She said that in Grande Prairie there wasn't any snow! She had come for five days to fill a spot at the local bank in McLennan. She liked to have peanut butter on her toast in the morning!

## Tuesday, March 7

☺ Maureen phoned at 10:05 a.m. She was inquiring about our bed and breakfast. She had seen our place on her previous trips to McLennan.  She was a teacher that goes from school to school, along with another teacher, Ben. She was considering traveling all the way to Peace River if she couldn't get any lodging in the area. She'll talk it over with Ben and get back to us tomorrow.

## Wednesday, March 8

☻ Sue phoned at 8:10 p.m. to cancel out her reservation for this weekend. Apparently the hockey team had booked up hotel rooms in High Prairie that had already been paid for.

## Thursday, March 9

☻ Debra and her 15 year old son, Doug, showed up at 3:00 p.m. They had driven all the way from Claresholm which is 800 km south of Donnelly. Both of them were very impressed with the place. They enjoyed watching sports on the big screen TV.

## Friday, March 10

Debra's neighbor decided to come and spend the weekend with us also. They were having a game of pool when I came in. They were both avid horseback riders and enjoyed barrel racing. Debra was considering going pro! Only thirteen people were selected from over 100 people. She had won enough cheques at competitions, so it was something that she was considering. They left to be at the opening ceremonies of the provincial hockey tournament by 7:00 p.m. It had cooled down enough that Debra was plugging in her truck.

## Saturday, March 11

☻ 10:00 p.m. John flew all the way from Florida to speak at the Falher arena about evolution and creation. Susan and her three kids drove from Fort St. John to listen to him. They were excited to be staying in the same place as the speaker. Apparently he was quite well-known.

☺

## Sunday, March 12

☻ The phone rang at 5:00 p.m. It was Lucien, Lucienne's brother, wishing to book up the double room for the big birthday party coming up at the end of March. I hoped that the weather wouldn't turn bad for them. Nobody likes driving through snowstorms.

## Monday, March 13

☻ 10:00 p.m. Vince stayed for one night. He was thinking about forming a Christian private school in McLennan. He wanted to start out small and then slowly increase the student population.

## Thursday, March 16

The Busy Bee Motel in McLennan phoned us with a young oil rig family, wishing to stay with us for several days or more. They were from Stony Plain. Michael's job involved capping the oil well by paving the cement and cleaning it up. He also prepared sites for the installation of hoses and other lines. His wife Lorraine took care of their two year old daughter Isabelle. Isabelle liked playing with the different toys that I got for her. Her favorite toys were the big balls. Michael parked his two big trucks and trailers in our ample-sized parking lot.

☺

# Friday, March 17

☻ The Busy Bee Motel phoned us again at 8:00 p.m. This time it was an older couple all the way from Yellowknife, wanting to spend the night with us. As it turned out, Doug had actually taught Roger back in the 1970s, in Donnelly! He had traveled twelve hours to come and visit a former teacher friend of his, who was dying of cancer in McLennan. They went right to sleep.

# Saturday, March 18

☺ The Busy Bee Motel phoned us at 11:20 a.m. There was a lady needing a room, but she was allergic to pets. We allow pets here and have pets of our own, so she never came.

Michael, the oil rig fellow, spent a lot of time doing his work on the computer. Everyone seemed to be trying to get over a cold.

# Sunday, March 19

Isabelle's eyes opened up as wide as saucers when Alex, our cockatiel was put on her head! She didn't know what to think. Lorraine called for Michael to quickly take a picture! Isabelle fed Cheerios to the hamster Cutie, and pet Pebi, the dwarf bunny. She was quite upset when the animals had to go have a nap! Lorraine used one of our sleighs to give Isabelle a ride around the property.

# Monday, March 20

Spring is officially here! Lorraine has had enough of being away from home for two weeks. Mom is always the boss, so tonight will be their last night here. Michael said that he would be back to pick up his trailer, sometime next week. I gave Isabelle one of the Usborne books about the brown pony. They left a nice card for us, thanking us for our hospitality.

# Tuesday, March 21

☻ The phone rang at 12:30 p.m. Heinz, the local honey producer phoned. He had four fellows from Edmonton coming to resurface his cement floor in his warehouse in Guy. They would probably be staying for three nights, starting with tonight. Sure enough, after driving four and a half hours, Dwayne, Rod, Bill, and Hank showed up 9:40 p.m. Their last job was at West Edmonton Mall. They were redoing the floor of the wave pool, and around the Ice Palace. One of the reasons why their company was chosen was because it offered a 25 year warranty. It was quite the process to remove the old finish, then to put on a top quality finish for over 77 000 sq ft!

# Wednesday, March 22

☺ The fellows were gone by 6:30 a.m. and did not come back until 10:20 p.m. It was a very tiring day for them. Some of them watched TV for a bit before heading off to bed.

## Thursday, March 23

☻ The phone rang at 5:05 p.m. It was Greg from Saskatchewan phoning about prices at our place. He and his wife are coming up this way to give a presentation on geothermal heating. The dentist in Falher, and the McLennan senior's facility, are going to be using the warmth of the earth to heat and cool their buildings.

## Friday, March 24

Some hockey team players from Berwyn stayed the night. The ones that had girlfriends went to a hotel. Roger enjoyed talking about hockey with them.

## Saturday, March 25

☻ The doorbell rang at 3:15 p.m. There clustered around the doorway was snow-white haired Lucien, with two moms and five children, ranging in age from eight to thirteen. They had driven all the way from Sundre and Rocky Mountain House to celebrate their great auntie's 80th birthday. Lucien insisted on paying for the two rooms for the gang. He was disappointed that he had already paid for a room in Falher. He would have rather stayed with us! The five youngsters wasted no time in trying out all of the activities. Their favorite was the sport stacking section. They had sport stacking at their school. They did not want to leave for the birthday party! One of the boys complained that the other boy didn't flush the toilet. He said that there was a log floating around.

Boys will be boys! The kids were pestering their moms to leave the party all night, so that they could return and play at Itlldo Place. They arrived back at 9:55 p.m. The eight year old asked Roger how he got the money to pay for all of the stuff!

## Sunday, March 26

☺ By 10:00 a.m., all the sleeping bags and luggage had been packed up and farewells were given. They were off to Falher to visit more with their family, before heading back home.

## Monday, March 27

☻ The phone rang at 6:55 p.m. It was Greg confirming that he, his wife, and three kids would be coming for April 7th and 8th.

## Tuesday, March 28

☻ The phone rang at 3:45 p.m. It was Stuart from the Smoky River Regional Development office. He suggested that we advertise more with a sign at the Donnelly Corner junction. He also wanted to book a room for a camera man who would be videotaping people and the area for the Kraft Hockeyville contest. Falher could win $50 000 to improve the arena and $10 000 for the children's hockey teams.

☺

# Wednesday, March 29

☻ The phone rang at 3:45 p.m. It was Busy Bee Travel, checking up to see if Trent, the camera man had a reservation for tonight. Trent popped in for a few moments before heading back to set up for the big event in Falher. He videotaped the crowds of hockey supporting fans that were in the gymnasium of the local school, as they heard that Falher had made it to the next round. Over 450 communities were applying to become Hockeyville of Canada, and now the judges had narrowed it down to 50 communities! Trent was busy interviewing people and did not get back until 10:00 p.m. He went to bed right away.

# Thursday, March 30

We were all booked for this weekend with presenters arriving for the trade show. Pierre and Pierrette were the first to come. Pierre proudly announced that he was 78 years old. They sold pinecone jewelry! If you slice open an unopened pinecone, you will see some interesting designs. Roger bought Leslie and I some earrings, a souvenir spoon, and a necklace. One of their daughters died of breast cancer. She gave up her baby to some millionaires. Their other two daughters decided to use and sell Mannatech health products. One of them lives in New Zealand now, so they don't get to see her too often.

Darren was representing a western magazine. He ended up sleeping on the sofa bed. He didn't mind where he slept as long as he had a spot to sleep. All the rooms in the local hotels were filled up.

## Friday, March 31

Nancy lived in the Peace area, but she wanted to be close to Falher for the weekend. She was a director with the Peace River tourism. Nancy might give our number to another lady who was thinking about starting up a bed and breakfast near Berwyn.

# April

## Saturday, April 1

Jerry and Trudy liked staying at our place because they didn't have to worry about their petting zoo animals in our yard, compared to a motel parking lot. The kids at the trade show loved to pet their various animals like a goat, chicken, turkey, lamb, guinea pig, rabbit, llama, and pig. He had some chinchillas that he was going to sell because they needed it to be warm and they were quite noisy. It was a chilly day once again to be set up outside with little protection. It took time to feed all the babies. Even at night he had to warm up bottles for them! Jerry had to rush back to his farm near Edmonton because of a sick goat, so he only stayed one night.

## Sunday, April 2

Gilbert, a French speaking native of Nova Scotia, said that he might stay with us for a couple of weeks. He moved around Alberta, depending on where he could get a job. He might work for Roger.

☺

## Monday, April 3

The principal of the local school came over to see where a good spot would be, to put up a school advertising sign on our property. With all of the highway regulations about putting up signs, it was easier to ask the owners of land for permission to put up signs. He would probably set it up for the fall, and then the next summer, we could use it to advertise specials for our bed and breakfast.

## Tuesday, April 4

☻ Emile and Candace popped in at 9:00p.m. They had just got back from Grande Prairie where they had watched a hockey game. Emile played some guitar and Roger played his keyboard. Tomorrow they are going to be visiting with some youth who are volunteering in the area, to see if things are going okay.

## Wednesday, April 5

A man from British Columbia came to check out our place. He was considering moving here, and might need a place to stay.

## Friday, April 7

☻ Greg and his family showed up at 9:50 p.m. They had phoned at 7:05 p.m. to say that they were still setting up for the big geothermal heating demonstration day on Saturday.

His three small kids wasted no time in quietly exploring the place, before going to bed in the bunk bed room. The girls wanted to share a bed.

## Saturday, April 8

Greg was saying that the geothermal technology came from Europe. It costs about $20 000 for a 1 500 sq ft home. The system is both for heating and air conditioning. It is pretty neat to hear about how heat energy can be stored and later used to heat up buildings at a constant temperature, and with no cold spots! His power bill to run his motors cost about $500 a year. Most of the crowd came at 10:00 a.m. He said that it was fairly busy. His kids were all excited about coming back here. They said that it was way better than a motel! They liked to play air hockey and Twister the most.

## Sunday, April 9

Greg's open house brought in so many inquiries that he had to stay one more night!

## Thursday, April 13

George and Sue from Fort St. John, stopped by for an hour's break. Sue was sick with that awful flu that was going around and needed to lie down. George decided that they had better head on home, because he was afraid that he would get sick and then we would have two sick people.

# Tuesday, April 18

☻ 6:30 p.m. Pedro and Priscilla were in Donnelly researching historical churches. Pedro was from Spain! They were interested in smaller churches that were abandoned or very small and in need of restoration.

# Saturday, April 22

Bob from Vanderhoof, British Columbia, arrived for his three week stay. He left his family temporarily, to start a new job at the local food store. He needed to find a place that his family would like and learn the ropes of being manager. He was also a cousin to a teacher living in town!

# Tuesday, April 25

Steve and Beth stopped by to check out our place. They thought that it would be a great place to stay if they had kids.

# Sunday, April 28

Danée returned to Donnelly to do more Métis research at the genealogical library. This time she stayed for four nights! She took her laptop with her from 9 to 5.

# May

## Friday, May 5

Lily and her family came from Edson for a family reunion. There were twelve people and one dog! Some stayed in a motor home. They were happy that the weather was cooperating!

## Saturday, May 6

I got an e-mail booking from Jessica again. She and her husband Philip want to come for two nights this coming week. It is always nice to visit with them.

## Sunday, May 7

☺ The phone rang at 7:20 a.m. It was Anthony inquiring about our rooms. He came over 15 minutes later. His first words upon entering our place were, "Sweet, sweet!" In no time at all, he had paid for a week and was in bed. He worked on the pipeline and needed to be at work at 7:30 p.m. for the night shift.

# Wednesday, May 10

☻Jessica and Philip arrived at 7:50 p.m. Jessica extended her arms into the usual hug. They were both such nice people! The schools that Jessica works for wanted her to come in May this year instead of June. Parents are quite busy in June and don't always have two hours to come to a meeting to discuss their child's speech problems. Jessica wanted to check up on her e-mails to see if she was going to have a meeting concerning a certain child. She was not having any luck with her computer, so I offered to let her use mine. Philip came upstairs too, to see if he could fix my daughter's computer which wouldn't dial up to the internet. Philip worked for two hours to get it all set up. He even created an e-mail account for Leslie with hotmail! It was past 11:00 p.m. before everyone went to bed.

# Thursday, May 11

Anthony arrived back from his night shift, just as Jessica and Philip were having their breakfast. Philip had work to do all day on his computer. He is a professor at the University of Alberta in political science. It turned out that Philip taught and wrote a reference for a Japanese fellow I met at the Chicoutimi University in Quebec, back in 1988! Both Nobuaki and I were taking a six week course to improve our French. Nobuaki's goal is to travel to every country! He is now a professor himself in Japan. What a small world! Jessica and Philip went out for supper and for a walk around Falher, to see all the decorations put up for the Hockeyville TV contest. There were hockey skates, hockey jerseys, hockey gardens, hockey banners, and hockey pictures everywhere. Falher was one of the top 25 contestants.

☻ Trent and his Québécois buddy Jean, stopped by at 6:00 p.m. They travel to paper mills all across the country to sell and repair parts. They are gone most of the year. Usually when they first go to a paper mill, the owners don't want to buy anything from them because the way they think is if something isn't broken, why change it. The first trip is to plant the idea and then on their second visit, they get more sales. Paper mills run 24/7 and make a tremendous amount of money per hour. Production is only halted if really necessary.

☻ Joan phoned at 12:40 p.m. to book a room for two nights. It is for a census lady who is coming from Edmonton for tomorrow.

## Friday, May 12

☻ Bianca arrived at 7:05 p.m., moments after Anthony left for his night shift. Anthony is a quiet person who watches a bit of TV and sleeps. We hardly see him. He is going to be a wet duck tonight with all of the rain coming down! Bianca was wearing her census identification tag and a cheerful grin as she came in. She is hoping to get a job this fall as a French teacher. There were about 70 people in her graduating class from La Faculté St. Jean in Edmonton. She was pretty excited about her convocation coming up. The students were from British Columbia, Alberta, Saskatchewan and the North West Territories. Bianca saw an ad in the Edmonton Journal for census taking people and decided to apply. It was very good money and with all of her expenses paid for. She was not impressed with the rental car that she was supposed to use on the wet and muddy country roads.

## Saturday, May 13

Bianca is an amazing 3D puzzle maker! After her breakfast, she worked on the Notre Dame puzzle that had been stumping me for a year, and within an hour and a half, she had pretty well assembled it all. Wow! What a smart gal! She should have no problem getting a job as a French teacher. Bianca was relieved that the dogs she encountered on the farm were all friendly. Some were too friendly and didn't want her to leave. She had to back out of those yards very carefully. Bianca didn't know why the census envelopes were hand delivered here, yet were mailed in the city.

## Sunday, May 14

☺Stephane pulled into our yard at 1:55 p.m. He was on-call for his oil company, and came to check out the place. He spoke in French most of the time and easily spent 30 minutes here. He has worked in Africa and Europe in the oil industry. He thought that it was very important for people to travel around the world, especially children, so that people are more aware of others and less likely to be prejudiced. He left, saying that he would be back some day with his family. He was very impressed!

Anthony paid for two more days. After that, he is off to go back home for a while. His next work place is Beaverlodge.

# Monday, May 15

☻ Semant rang the doorbell at 7:00 p.m. He was with his wife. They were originally from India, but now live in Edmonton. They were able to immigrate sooner than most people, because Semant took a course to learn how to speak French. Semant was an exporter and was in the area to buy peas and possibly honey. There was a 33 000-tonne ship that they had to fill up, before the ship headed back to India. We had a delightful time playing badminton, pool, and playing the piano and keyboard. They didn't think that we were charging enough for the rooms!

# Wednesday, May 17

☻ It was just starting to get a little dark at 9:45 p.m., when a white van came into the yard. It didn't park on the brick parking lot. It turned out that is was Kayla-Lynn and her fiancé. They had just gotten engaged and wanted to spend one night here in celebration of their upcoming elopement. He proposed to her on one knee, after she had just been stung by a bee and was crying, saying that everything was going to be alright. I taught little Kayla-Lynn when she was in grade one! Who is feeling old now!! Kayla-Lynn had also bought a white puppy off of me in December. She changed his name from Sax to Buddy. Unfortunately he got the parvovirus when he was on the farm and died in March. She showed me some scrapbook pictures of him. He looked like he was well-loved. Kayla-Lynn also showed me her engagement ring. It was a pretty ring with three diamonds on it. Her fingers were too swollen up to wear it though. She gave me a hug when she saw how I had decorated the room for them. They had fun playing badminton and pool, before settling down to a good movie.

## Thursday, May 18

Steven was working for Alphonse. They were house builders who worked in Falher and Donnelly. Steven was all the way from Newfoundland! He needed a place to stay for a couple of weeks. He will be busy working long hours and taking advantage of the long days of sunshine.

## Friday, May 19

☻ The phone rang at 5:35 p.m. My call display showed that it was a cell phone number from British Columbia. It was actually a family of three from Penticton, looking for two rooms. They were in town, to attend the high school graduation ceremony. Dennis, the step-dad said that there were 44 graduating students and over 600 guests! That was definitely showing support! Dennis worked on off-shore oil rigs. They had to learn to really get along with each other, because even when they had time off, they were still on the rig. Boats had to be aware of these floating islands, because the rigs are never dissembled. The boat would be the loser out of the two. Julie, the mom thought that our place was very cool! Two more friends of the family came over to watch an exciting game of the playoffs on the big-screen TV. The Edmonton Oilers were one more step closer to winning the Stanley Cup!

## Saturday, May 20

Dennis and his son Martin had lots of fun on the air hockey game and playing badminton. There was lots of laughter. They must have stayed up late last night, because they didn't get up until 11:45 a.m.! It was too bad that it rained today. All the beautiful dresses and suits had to be covered up.

## Sunday, May 21

☺ Julie said that when they come back, they would be sure to stay with us again. They left to go back home at 10:35 a.m.

## Tuesday, May 23

☻ The phone rang at 1:40 p.m. It was Merissa phoning to see if we had any rooms available for the July 15th weekend. There was going to be a big 50th anniversary in our area. Since Roger was in Peace River at the time, answering on his cell phone, he couldn't confirm that date. When he called back later, Merissa had already booked up the room somewhere else.

## Wednesday, May 24

☻ Tina phoned at 2:00 p.m., wanting to know more about our place, like if we had a kitchenette, which we do. She had stopped by on the weekend, but nobody was home. She was planning on staying a week with us in August.

# Sunday, May 28

☻ The doorbell rang two different times tonight. One at 7:25 p.m., it was a doctor from the area, coming to check out our place. She had always been curious about it. She might come with her family.

☻ The second time it was at 9:00 p.m. Mr. Lebreque first knocked on the knocker and then he rang the bell. Mrs. Lebreque was amazed at how fast I answered the door! I had just been watering the plants and was close by. Mr. Lebreque's family is in Iowa, and he hadn't seen his family in close to 40 years! Everyone was in their 60s to 80s! They wanted to know if they could have a potluck supper here too. They were quite certain that this place would be ideal. They left promising to phone tomorrow with an answer either way. At 9:50 p.m., Mr. Lebreque phoned to say, "It'll do for our Itlldo Place!" They were such a nice couple. I hope that they will have many happy memories for the June 22-26 family reunion!

# Tuesday, May 30

☺ The doorbell rang at 8:30 a.m. Darren, Justin, and Ruel were there to check out our place. They were working on the new senior's facility that was going up in McLennan, and needed a place to stay for awhile. The footings were done and now they had to backhoe the dirt around it. Ruel was one of the plumbers for part of the $7 million project. They will come back tonight. They came at 8:35 p.m. After visiting for a bit, Justin the boss and Ruel, went outside on the deck to have a cigarette and to chat on their cell phones. Darren, the youngest one, had fun playing badminton, air hockey and hockey with us.

## Wednesday, May 31

☺ The fellows were gone by 7:20 a.m. They did not come back until 9:45 p.m. I was very glad to see them, because our water heater's pressure relief valve was not working, and hot steamy water was flowing everywhere. Between the four of us, we were able to phone the Home Hardware owner at his home. He opened up the shop for me to buy another valve. Ruel was able to change the valves within 10 minutes. I gave him a thank you hug, along with a card with some money for a nice supper. He didn't want any payment for his services. Justin was explaining about the cons and pros about having hot water on-demand. Justin thinks that instead of an eighty-five gallon tank like what we have now, a sixty gallon tank would be better. I decided to buy a Bosch heat-on-demand unit, to use during the warm months and a water tank for the cold months of the year. Tonight will be their last night, since they were able to rent a house in McLennan. It is located only a minute away from their work site.

# June

## Thursday, June 1

☻ The doorbell rang at 10:30 p.m. It was an 84 year old man who was a former boxer, with his wife. They had driven all the way from Yellowknife, North West Territories. They had been looking for a place to stay before Peace River, and we were the first vacancy. They were very relieved! The drive down had been eventful enough with some speeders, bears, deer, and buffalo to contend with. Most of the way was flat with trees and wildflowers along the way. Where they come from there is a top security diamond mine. Supplies can only be brought in during the winter because of the soft muskeg. They were going to Edmonton to visit their nephew who was in critical care at the hospital. He was hit by an 18 year old girl who swerved her car to avoid a dog, and ended up running over him. She panicked and tried to take off, but a car blocked her way. Their nephew was still trapped underneath the car. The car had to be lifted up to get him out, leaving him with both lungs collapsed, broken ribs and several other injuries. So far he had survived four days on life support systems. He has a wife and kids. The great-grandpa and Roger stayed up until midnight watching boxing on the TV.

## Friday, June 2

☻ Lyle arrived at our place at 8:35 p.m. He had driven all the way from Sherwood Park to Peace River, only to find out that there were no vacancies there, neither in Nampa nor in Falher. Good thing we were able to come to his rescue! He worked for Alberta Transport and was going to be in a golf tournament the next day, in Eaglesham. He was pleasantly surprised with our place. He particularly enjoyed playing memorized classical pieces on my Young Chang baby grand. He recently purchased a grand piano and plays daily on it whenever he can. Lyle might bring his family for a visit one day. Lyle particularly enjoyed the meal at the local confectionary. The Saskatoon crumble pie was delicious! He really liked to chat with us!

## Saturday, June 3

☺ We awoke at 7:45 a.m. to the strains of the piano playing. Lyle couldn't resist another practice before heading out to his tournament. Lyle also finished more of the 3D puzzle of Notre Dame Cathedral in Paris. He took some of our business cards for his acquaintances.

Edward and Jenn slept over for one night. They were in town visiting their daughter, whose place was too small for them to stay with.

☺

# Sunday, June 4

☻ More of Mr. Labreque's family came at 2:20 p.m., to check out Itlldo Place, for the family reunion in a couple of weeks. They are going to be splitting the bill. It still looks good!

☻ The phone rang at 8:05 p.m. Daisy from Grande Prairie was wondering what our prices were, and if we had any openings for the July 1 weekend. Her family wanted to attend the big Guy reunion. Daisy will phone her daughter in Calgary and get back to us tomorrow.

# Monday, June 5

Daisy never phoned us back, but a lady from Guy's welcoming committee phoned to get information on our rates for the last weekend of the month.

☻ A couple from Kelowna also stopped by at 3:30 p.m., to check out our place. Dale was over six feet tall! I think that he was looking for a king's size bed.

# Tuesday, June 6

☺ The phone rang at 8:25 a.m. It was Mitchell, standing right outside our home! He took a quick tour before saying that he would be back after packing up from his hotel room in the next town. He was not impressed with the cleanliness of the hotel. The microwave was dirty, someone had left rotten milk in the fridge and he was afraid of getting robbed. He worked the grave shift in the oil patch. He has a wife and three youngsters at home in Saskatchewan on a cattle farm. We gave him a discounted price for staying twenty days with us.

## Wednesday, June 7

Mitchell called up to me to get some help boosting his truck. He had switched his lights to manual so that he could have light while branding his calves, and had forgotten to turn off his lights because he was so tired after work. My van's battery was in an awkward position, so he went to the local repair shop to get a boost. Mitchell was lucky, because he was just closing up for the night! Mitchell enquired if some more of his buddies could come and stay with us.

☻ Roger phoned me at 7:05 p.m. to say that two ladies were coming Friday night, and two fellows were coming, starting on Sunday night, for seven to ten nights. Things are really starting to book up!

## Thursday, June 8

The two ladies decided not to come. One didn't want to sleep on a bunk bed! They had some work to do at the local bank in Falher.

☻ Jubal phoned at 3:45 p.m. to ask questions about our internet dial-up. He was happy about our discounted price for staying a week.

☺

# Friday, June 9

Dean and his son Chris were from Nanaimo, British Columbia. Dean lived in McLennan twenty years ago and was bringing Chris to see where he used to live. Dean even remembered this place being constructed! There were quite a few fellows working here.

# Saturday, June 10

☻ 10:30 p.m. Bev and her thirteen year old son Dale had driven as much as they were going to today. They were journeying from Anchorage, Alaska and going all the way to Texas, for her son to go to military school for the summer. Her son looked very young and was a bit anxious about the school. His mom was proud of him but had mixed feelings as well.

# Sunday, June 11

☻ The doorbell rang at 8:10 p.m. It was Jubal and his working partner Danton, from Edmonton. They were water engineers who would be staying with us for a week, while they checked out the water canals that supply water to the local communities. They were going to be taking pictures and determining how much it would cost to repair them. Jubal and Roger took a tour outside. Jubal liked what we have done to the place.

☺

## Monday, June 12

☺ The phone rang at 9:30 a.m. and 9:45 a.m., both wanting rooms for tonight. We were all full though. Another potential customer came at 10:00 p.m., looking for a room for one night. He didn't want to go on a foamie and sleeping bag. Rooms are all booked up in the area.

Jubal asked about his being able to download pictures from his digital camera. His memory card was all full. He will have to go to The Stop in Falher tomorrow and buy another one. Jubal had a phoning card to make long distance calls with. He liked to chat with Roger.

## Tuesday, June 13

Jubal and Danton had a long day examining the canals and taking pictures. Danton worked on his computer in his room when they came back, and Jubal went outside on the swing to get caught up in some reading. He liked the view.

## Wednesday, June 14

Danton informed us that tomorrow would be their last day. He is needed back in Edmonton at the office. He will be recommending us to the others involved in this project.

☺

## Thursday, June 15

Jubal purchased two books from my Usborne selection. He chose A Tale of Two Cities, and Find the Duck! We said our goodbyes in the morning, before heading out ourselves.

As I was cleaning out Jubal's room later on in the evening, I noticed an electronic card game for playing Solitaire. I e-mailed Jubal to see if it belonged to him.

## Wednesday, June 21

A six member band all the way from Montreal stayed with us. They were hired by the local radio station, to perform for the St. Jean Baptist day celebrations going on in the area. They practiced a bit on our dance floor and on the couches. They were really good! They signed a poster for us. They were glad that we spoke French.

## Thursday, June 22

☻ The Labreque family arrived at 10:30 p.m. Everyone was all smiles as the introductions and tours were made. Teressa the grandmother, had been raised in the Girouxville area, grew up and went to Alaska where she fell in love with an American GI. In Alaska, Teressa lived in a trailer where she had to put towels over the windows in the summer, in order to darken the room so that she could get to sleep. She still remembers staying up late writing letters to home, then being tired the next day. They moved to Idaho where they had two daughters. Simone and Rachelle had come to the area for a visit when they were about six years old, so they were quite happy to reconnect with family members in this area. It wasn't long before everyone was in bed. They had been up since 6:30 a.m. Roger and I moved tables and chairs onto the dance floor for the family potluck supper. Thirty guests are expected tomorrow afternoon and into the night.

## Friday, June 23

The family reunion was quite the success with lots of talking, hugging and getting to know each other again. The piano got a work out too! Simone happily handed out the famous Idaho Spud chocolate bars. Clean-up was a breeze since everyone took home their own pot and disposable dishes were used. Roger entertained our guests with his piano playing, after everyone else had left. One of the self-composed songs that he played was called, *I Met a Girl at the Donnelly Fair*. Simone said that in Idaho, there is also a place called Donnelly!

## Saturday, June 24

The Labreque's went to visit the Girouxville Museum. They didn't see the famous five-legged squirrel, but they did enjoy it. The girls were surprised to see the creek where their grandma went swimming in! They also went to McLennan's Birdwalk and went to a birthday party. They really enjoyed their visit!

A man in a black car pulled up at noon wanting to stay until July 3. Unfortunately we were all booked up.

# Sunday, June 25

The Labreque's had a good day in McLennan. They brought back a placemat about the Alaska Highway that was at the museum. One of their relatives had made up the display! On their way back to Donnelly, they particularly enjoyed the sunset. It lasted a long time. They even took a picture of it when they reached Donnelly. Rachelle wanted a copy of a note I had up by my Usborne collection of books. It said, "This is wild… I cluod nto blveiee taht I cluod aulaclty uesdnatnrd waht I was rdanieg

## THE PAOMNNEHEL PWEOR OF THE HMUAN MNID

Aoccdrnig to a rsreearche at Cmabrigde Uinervtisy, it deosn't mttaer in waht oredr the ltteers in a wrod are, the olny iprmoatnt tihng is taht the frist and lsat ltteer be in the rghit pclae. The rset can be a taotl mses and you can sitll raed it wouthit a porbelm. Tihs is bcuseae the huamn mnid deos not raed ervey lteter by istlef, but the wrod as a wlohe.

Amzanig huh?

Harv

☻ The Busy Bee Motel in McLennan phoned at 5:10 p.m. to see if we had room for a lady who was due to come in late tonight. We had to turn the offer down, as we are still full.

# Monday, June 26

The Labreque's decided to go back to Edmonton to catch their airplane by the Slave Lake route. They hope to return to visit here one day. Three different family members wanted to pay for the rooms. It ended up being their cousin Pierre! Pierre will pay us when he comes back from holidays in a week!

## Tuesday, June 27

When I was taking my dog for a walk, a fellow on the street asked me if we had any rooms available for tonight. His acquaintance Stanley, needed a room after supper. He never showed up.

☻ At 7:00 p.m., Kirk pulled up to our place to check it out. He took a business card.

☻ At 9:10 p.m., the Garants phoned to confirm that they still had a room for a week, starting on Thursday.

☻ At 10:25 p.m. the phone rang. It was Henri, a fellow who took care of the fairgrounds in town, wondering if we had room for his buddy Hank. Hank worked for a road upkeep company and didn't want to drive two hours in the rain to go home, then another two hours to be back in Donnelly by six in the morning. He came and ended up chatting with Roger before heading off to bed. Hank moved up here in 1969. He has been working at his present job for eight years now. He has a big territory to cover, putting in long days and avoiding moose, bear, and deer. Sometimes he has to travel all night. His daughter lives back home and just last week her collie pup got run over and ended up with a broken leg. Apparently there were scuffles between Hank and another cattle rancher. It turned out that the neighbor's dog kept coming over and killing Hank's calves, so he shot the dog.

The neighbor ended up beating up the pup. Hank's middle son's dog was a good herder, but he turned mean so he sent him off to a lady down the way. Hank ended up getting the dog back when the lady sold her cows!

## *Wednesday, June 28*

☻ The phone rang at 3:30 p.m. It was the secretary calling to make another reservation for the water engineer company. Danton and Jubal who stayed with us two weeks ago had recommended us. This time it was for Carson. He will come July 4 and 5.

☻ The phone rang at 7:05 p.m. The Summers saw us on the Travel Alberta internet site and wanted to sightsee around the Smoky River region. The two adults and two kids will come July 3.

☻ 9:05 p.m. Andrew and Rosemary were fed up with the rain, and were very happy to see our sign. They had driven all the way from Whitehorse. Andrew was very talkative about how beautiful the scenery was in the Yukon and how many different zones there are. He should be a tourist guide! They were on their way to Saskatchewan. He also spoke passionately about the need to look after the environment. Simple things like having a two minute shower with the water heater temperature on low, not buying bottled water, unplugging electrical appliances when not in use, to recycling. Rosemary mentioned that in the oceans, there is so much plastic and waste that these 'islands' can be seen from outer space. Not something to be proud about.

Hank phoned to see if he could stay another night. There was more work to do then he had thought. He arrived at 10:55 p.m. Henri was breaking three of his horses. One was quite the challenge!

## Thursday, June 29

Mitchell is still here, he pleasantly gave a wave as he carried out his business. His last day will be July 2. His oil rig employer keeps on finding more work for him to do. Mitchell was anxious to get back home to see his family.

The Garants arrived from Airdrie. They are staying a week with us. They are here to visit with family. Lucienne is recovering from breast cancer. She was a former teacher in Falher, who is now cherishing life and her family. As it turned out, her sister Denise, who was also a teacher, was once married to Roger's cousin. Lucienne's other sister Madeline, was the OR nurse when our daughter Leslie was born! What a small world! Lucienne's mother and husband both loved to play on my baby grand piano. The family enjoyed singing along too. Ralph even brought a dozen piano books. Denise must have mentioned that we had a piano to him, before he left home.

## Friday, June 30

☺ The phone rang at 8:30 a.m. and again at 9:00 a.m. It was Katherine from British Columbia, reserving a room for her family at the end of July. Katherine babysat our daughter for a bit six years ago! There will be a lot of visiting going on! The Garants liked looking at our garden areas, but the mosquitoes were really biting. There were a lot of mosquitoes because of the rain this year.

☻ 10:00 p.m. Janessa and Adrian decided that it was late enough to be traveling in the rain. They lived in Calgary in the same neighborhood as my brother! Their destination this trip was Fort Nelson, for the Canada Day celebrations. They will perform magic tricks. Roger and I got to see first hand some of their card tricks. It was all in the movement of the hands. They were kind to sign one of their posters for us to hang up on the wall. Janessa is interested in genealogy, so she might come back to do some research at the local library.

# July

## Saturday, July 1

Lucienne and Ralph ate breakfast here today, because a lot of the restaurants were closed for Canada Day.

## Sunday, July 2

Mitchell packed up and left today. He left a bunch of food in the fridge that I cleaned out. Our dogs enjoyed the meat, the rabbit and hamster enjoyed the vegetables!

The Garants had a family piano concert here tonight. They liked to play music from the seventies and eighties.

## Monday, July 3

● The Summers arrived at 8:30 p.m. Gary had a sore back. He and his wife and two kids had driven through British Columbia for a holiday. They were a quiet and nice family who played games in the games room and watched TV.

☺

## Tuesday, July 4

The Summers slept in, then were gone by noon. The kids enjoyed sleeping in the bunk bed room.

☻ Carson arrived at 8:00 p.m. He was here to examine the canal bridges from McLennan to Girouxville. He determines which bridges need to be replaced or what work needs to be done for each one, to bring it up to standards.

## Wednesday, July 5

Carson left early in the morning to go work in the rain. The mosquitoes are thriving in this type of weather!

## Thursday, July 6

Carson was going to finish up his work here and then head back to Edmonton later on today.

## Saturday, July 8

The first two of eight people arrived today for the funeral of their 81 year old mom/grandma. They are here until the 11th. Adrien was quite the character telling jokes and telling tall tales! For example- There was a bakery in France and two tourists were watching this big Italian rolling pizza dough on his stomach. The woman said, "That's gross!" The Italian replied, "Wait until I do doughnuts!" Another joke was- There were two old eighty-eight year old farmers who had one too many at the bar. They stumbled across a whorehouse and figured that this might be the last time that they would be able to have a woman. They were led to the bedrooms where a blow-up doll was in each room. The ladies thought that the old fellows wouldn't know the difference anyway. After, the two men compared notes on how it went. The first man said that he thought the lady was dead. He said that he talked to her, loved her and rubbed her but she didn't do anything. The second man said that he thought his lady was a witch. He said that he caressed her, loved her and bit her neck, then watched her fly out of the window! On a more mathematical note, 04:05:06 07/08/09 is five minutes and six seconds after 4 a.m. of July 8, 2009. 111 111 111 X 111 111 111=12 345 678 987 654 321. 98 765 432 X 9 = 888 888 888.

And the last one is:
If A B C D E F G H I J K L M N O P Q R S T U V W X Y Z

is represented as
1 2 3 4 5 6 7 8 9 10 11 12 13 14 15 16 17 18 19 20 21 22 23 24 25 26

Then HARDWORK is
8+1+18+4+23+15+18+11=98

And KNOWLEDGE is
11+14+15+23+12+5+4+7+5=96

But ATTITUDE is
1+ 20+20+9+20+21+4+5=100

☺

## Sunday, July 9

Jubal came back today for three nights to do more work on the canals. We might have an empty B&B when everyone leaves on the 12th! He needed a favour of duplicating 60 copies of some of his work that he couldn't get done at his office. He offered to pay for them.

Another couple arrived today for the funeral. Carmen and Luke visited a lot with Adrien and Sarah. Carmen's two daughters, and son-in-law will come tomorrow.

## Monday, July 10

The two daughters Monique and Francine, as well as Mark, arrived after the funeral. They didn't realize that they were tracking in mud on their dress shoes. They did not want to come in barefoot. Their dads kindly gave up their beds, and slept on the foamies with sleeping bags. Monique bought The Great Dinosaur Search Usborne book off of me, for her son. They were going to go to the Tyrell Museum in Drumheller and thought that he would enjoy it.

## Tuesday, July 11

Francine and Mark were pleasantly surprised to have slept well last night. Usually it takes them awhile to get to sleep. They were also impressed with how quiet it was here compared to Sherwood Park, and to not have their rambunctious children waking them up!

Jubal wanted me to e-mail him a clever e-mail that I had received. It's about rearranging the letters of some words, to become new words that make sense! For example, DORMITORY becomes DIRTY ROOM, DESPERATION becomes A ROPE ENDS IT, THE EYES become THEY SEE, THE MORSE CODE becomes HERE COME DOTS, SLOT MACHINES become CASH LOST IN ME, ELECTION RESULTS become LIES- LET'S RECOUNT, SNOOZE ALARMS become ALAS! NO MORE Z'S, THE EARTHQUAKES become THAT QUEER SHAKE, ELEVEN PLUS TWO becomes TWELVE PLUS ONE, and MOTHER-IN-LAW becomes WOMAN HITLER.

Halli e-mailed me for information about our bed and breakfast. She might come with her husband later on.

## Wednesday, July 12

☺ The funeral bunch headed out before 9:00 a.m. Carmen made sure that nothing was left behind! One of their license plates had the war veteran logo on it!

Jubal came back in the afternoon to have a shower and lunch. He took pictures of the place before leaving for Edmonton.

## Thursday, July 13

☻ An oil rig fellow came at 1:10 p.m. He inquired about our daily versus monthly rates.

## Saturday, July 15

Our last load of rocks for around the dugout came tonight. Roger's former school teacher stopped her car, to comment on how nice we were making the entrance to Donnelly.

Lisa, who works for Falher's alfalfa plant, helped to place some rocks with us, while she was waiting for a ride. Her truck had broken down.

## Sunday, July 16

A Japanese couple came to our place while we were having a marshmallow roast. The lady had to use our washroom. They thought that we had a very beautiful place. They were going to Fort Vermillion.

## Tuesday, July 18

Lisa honked at us while we were placing more rocks. She might come and stay with us in the winter. Right now she is in the McLennan's campsite.

## Wednesday, July 19

After swimming in the Peace River pool, I was in the steam room when the fellow who had been swimming in the same lane as my daughter and I, said that he knew my husband from hockey. He asked questions about our bed and breakfast too. We are getting quite well known!

## Thursday, July 20

We faxed a license application to have Grass Carp in our dugout. The fish are two pounds, and can reach over fifty pounds! They will eat the plants and algae in the water.

Mrs. Drouin phoned about our guests that are coming on the weekend. They will be here for Saturday and Sunday night. Mrs. Drouin knew me from a triathlon that I participated in four years ago. She loaned me a bicycle helmet. I had forgotten mine at home in all the excitement! Her husband was our accountant as well!

## Friday, July 21

A man stopped by to check out our place. He was from Grande Prairie but did not get along with his boss, so he was checking out the alternatives in our area. He liked small towns where the people are friendly. There was too much drug dealing going on in Grande Prairie.

We had some bricks delivered for a walking path around a flower garden, and some sidewalk blocks for around the firepit. The weather is over thirty degrees. Very hot work!

## Saturday, July 22

☺ Cindy arrived at 10:30 a.m. Her husband was in Roger's baseball tournament this weekend. She needed a cool place to work on her master's degree homework, with her dog tagging along. Her husband had brought their trailer down from Worsley to Winagami Lake to go camping, but Cindy hated swatting the mosquitoes! Cindy was a special education teacher and she also worked with German Mennonites. She was totally enthralled with our place. She thought that it was stunning, a real jewel, and she loved it! Her husband and sister came later to take her out for lunch. She decided then to book a room for tonight. She took some business cards to hand them out to people traveling up north.

☻ The phone rang at 1:00 p.m. It was our guests for the family reunion/anniversary this weekend. Claire knew Roger and was wondering if Roger was dyeing his hair yet! Claire, her husband Mike, and their two boys had come all the way from Quebec. She teased Roger about looking old! They were both in the same classes in high school.

## Sunday, July 23

The two boys were disappointed that they had to go visit their grandma in the nursing home in McLennan, instead of going on a paddleboat ride with us. They really enjoyed playing pool and both paid $5 each to own a stack of mini-sport stacking cups. Claire gave me a hug goodbye. They were looking forward to visiting the mountains.

Cindy came to say thank you for the nice visit. We were preparing the fire pit area for the sidewalk blocks. She was off to go watch her husband's last baseball game. She said that she would be in hot water if she didn't! Her cute dog was with her too.

☺

## Monday, July 24

As I was coming in with groceries, two fellows came to the door to see if we had room for a crew of six, for five to six weeks. We unfortunately couldn't help them because we were booked for most weekends already. One of the fellows remembered the place when it was a bar and restaurant!

## Tuesday, July 25

☻ The phone rang at 9:35 p.m. to see if we had any rooms available for this Thursday and Friday. It was for another funeral. The Edmonton people phoned five minutes later to book up two rooms. The well-respected head nurse in McLennan, died of breast cancer at the age of 52. She will be greatly missed.

## Wednesday, July 26

☺ The phone rang at 8:35 a.m. The people from Edmonton who phoned yesterday, were invited to stay with relatives, so they will not be coming to our place.

☻ The phone rang at 12:40 p.m. It was the doctor's wife in McLennan, phoning to get some information about our rooms. She wanted to know if they were on the ground floor and whether we had central air or not.

☺

# Thursday, July 27

☻ The phone rang at 1:30 p.m. It was a lady inquiring about our prices and where we were located.

Katherine and her husband Ken, along with their three boys came at 8:10 p.m. They had just driven 13 hours from Mission B.C.! Needless to say they had to use the washroom! They all wanted to stay in the double room. The boys had brought their own sleeping bags. Katherine wanted to see how much Leslie had grown since she had last seen her. Katherine was Leslie's babysitter many years ago! They left shortly after arriving, to go and see their nieces on their horses at the local gymkhana.

# Friday, July 28

Surprise, surprise, Claire and her two boys zoomed back to buy two standard size sport stacking cups for $23 each. Apparently they watched the DVD at their uncle's and now everyone was hooked on sport stacking!

Katherine mentioned to us as we were placing rocks by the fountain, that she wanted to pay us before she forgot. They were planning on leaving at 5:00 a.m. on Sunday morning! They really liked coming and going as they pleased, without feeling obligated to do what the rest of their family would like them to do, if they were staying with them. They were looking forward to seeing what our place would look like next year. Ken liked to stay up to watch TV and the boys liked playing at the pool table.

# Saturday, July 29

☺ At 11:55 a.m., a woman rang the doorbell. She had to use our washrooms. Ever since the Esso at Donnelly Corner shut down, there aren't too many places for travelers to have access to washrooms.

As Roger and I were laying sidewalk blocks by the fire pit, a lady pulled up asking if we wouldn't mind giving a duffel bag with clothes in it, to a fellow who would be coming through on Sunday. She didn't want to have to backtrack to give it to him. We do get funny requests!

Katherine thanked us greatly for our hospitality before setting their alarm clock for 3:55 a.m. They had a nice time visiting with family and friends. I thanked their boys for being so good. They beamed with pride!

# Sunday, July 30

☻ Chloe phoned at 7:50 p.m. There had been a death in her family and she wanted to know if she could stay and leave her puppy with us, while she attended the funeral. She'll phone us back to confirm her reservation.

# Monday, July 31

☻ The phone rang at 12:30 p.m. It was a local news reporter, wanting to take a picture of Roger and myself at our bed and breakfast, for the beautiful garden article that she was doing!

The phone rang at 6:30 p.m. It was Chloe phoning to say that she will be coming tomorrow night.

# August

## Tuesday, August 1

Chloe and Emilie arrived with their pup, which turned out to be a 100 pound Golden Lab mix! Good thing that he was friendly, although rather energetic and not wanting to heel! Both of the ladies were teachers from Fort McMurray. It took them six hours to drive here. The funeral is tomorrow, then another long drive back home.

☻ Hank rang the doorbell at 10:35 p.m. In Edmonton where he is from, the darkness outside would be equivalent to about 9:35 p.m. He apologized for arriving late. He got carried away talking with the owner of a honey producing plant in Guy, where he was hired to help work out problems of getting honey to not solidify. As a food scientist, he works out any problem with plants. At another job, he was hired to get gluten out of wheat.

## Wednesday, August 2

Hank left in such a hurry that he forgot his t-shirt in the washroom. He was supposed to come and pick it up, but he had to rush off to Edmonton. He might come another time to pick it up.

☻ Gwen and Heather arrived at 4:50 p.m. They were in the area to study the wildlife in their natural habitat of the water canal. They came prepared to tackle any weather condition, as well as the pesky mosquitoes! They set off for dinner and then didn't come back until dark. The wildlife that they saw included a red-tailed hawk, a coyote, and some frogs.

## Thursday, August 3

☺ On our answering machine at 10:30 a.m., we had a message from a dispatcher working at the government's office. She wanted to know if Premier Ralph Klein's pilots could spend the day at our bed and breakfast, while the premier was at his charity golf tournament. There is a rule that the pilots have to have a certain amount of sleep. Of course we were delighted with the news!

## Friday, August 4

Kylie and her two school-aged boys came all the way from Mayerthorpe, to participate in the local gymkhana going on at the fairgrounds. Kylie used to be a kindergarten aide. She loved working with that age group! When she got divorced, she had to sell her motorhome, so she needed a place to stay while her boys competed on their two horses.

☺

# Saturday, August 5

☺Kylie, Cedric and Sam were gone early in the morning to get ready to be in the 11:00 a.m. agricultural parade around town. Cedric and Sam waved as they passed on their horses. They were very fast at the events such as the keyhole and poles. Kylie said that she is fussy about where she will stay and that she absolutely loved it here. She was telling everyone about this place and took several business cards to hand out. She was surprised that some people didn't know what B&B stands for. She thought that we should advertise more! Kylie was pleased to see us watching her boys during the events.

# Sunday, August 6

●Anthony and Lynda were waxed and needed a place to stay at 9:30 p.m. They lived in Fort McMurray and were off to Prince George to buy an $80 000 truck. Anthony makes $180 000 a year as a carpenter. He puts up scaffolding and gets to work in the highly demanding building business. People pay on average $120 000 for a lot up there. Lynda works with children. They went to the local confectionary for their supper. They brought back some food to eat here.

# Monday, August 7

Our guests took some business cards to give to people who travel our way. They said that we would do better with signs on the highway. They left at noon and both waved as they took off on the highway. They were impressed with how nice and clean Itlldo Place was.

## Tuesday, August 8

☺ Today we had our first VIPs! We heard the airplane flying over us at 10:40 a.m., so we eagerly made our way to the Smoky River Regional airport. It is located just south of Donnelly. We watched as the plane carrying Premier Ralph Klein touched down and came to a stop by us. The local reporter and greeters were also there. A yellow helicopter landed shortly after, carrying officials who were looking at a proposed new roadway to link the Peavine- Métis settlement with McLennan. The cost had escalated to $6 million instead of $2.7 million, which was predicted two years ago. We were able to get pictures of Premier Ralph Klein and his pilots, before waiting for the pilots to secure the airplane. The King Air plane was 25 years old and would be sold for around $3 million, when the new aircraft arrives. It costs too much to keep the old planes up to safety standards. The pilots Dale and Peter had flown from Edmonton to Calgary, then up to Donnelly. It only took an hour to fly from Calgary. Dale had been a commercial pilot for seven years now. He said that it was quite easy to get your license, but it was another thing to land your first job. Usually they fly to Valleyview or Peace River. It didn't take them long to change into their shorts, then head to the local confectionary for a clubhouse sandwich. They slept for four hours and then I drove them back to the airport to wait for Premier Ralph Klein. We waited an hour before he got back from a charity golf tournament and dinner that was in Eaglesham. Peter kindly gave me some

Blue Diamond almonds and some bottled water from the plane. I was waiting to get the premier's autograph in my guest book. I held an umbrella over his head as he went to board the plane. He told a reporter that he always felt welcome in the North because, "All the real people lived there." He also thought that the Eaglesham golf course gets more beautiful every year.

☻ Jerry and Kyra were at Itlldo Place when I got back at 8:15 p.m. They were from Edmonton. Jerry had heard about us through relatives. They were impressed to know that we had the premier's pilots staying here! They were traveling around northern Alberta. Before leaving the area, they wanted to buy some honey in Falher, see the big bee and the live bee display at the tourist center. They were in bed by 9:20 p.m.

## Thursday, August 10

We had a pleasant surprise in the mail from Katherine who had stayed here with her family in July. It was a thank you card for having them. She complimented us on how beautiful we were making the place, and how the boys had enjoyed the toys and games.

## Friday, August 11

☻ The doorbell rang at 4:40 p.m. It was Rachelle, Stephen, and their toddler son Louis, along with their Yorkshire terrier from Quebec City, Quebec! Rachelle got a job in Falher as the new grade one French teacher. Their moving van broke down in Winnipeg Manitoba, so they needed a place to stay for a few nights. They felt very welcome and were happy with all the things to do here.

## Saturday, August 12

Rachelle and her family took off to go and visit Grande Prairie for the day. They were planning on leaving early tomorrow morning, so that they could be at their apartment before the moving van arrived.

## Sunday, August 13

☻ Sure enough the young family was off bright and early, only to return at 3:45 p.m. The moving van was still a day away. Rachelle's landlady phoned us at 2:00 p.m. to relay the message to us, since Rachelle didn't have a cell phone. Rachelle was amazed at how fast news spread in a small town. Stephen liked the lower taxes in Alberta. It was much lower than in Quebec. They moved here because they want their son to be bilingual and to be in a wealthy province where there are shorter wait times for doctor's appointments. I invited a grade two French teacher over to come and visit with them. She came from Quebec about 19 years ago. Rachelle wanted to know about furniture, grocery stores, banks, and how to learn English!

Roxanne, a pharmacist from Calgary, arrived just before supper. She was going to spend a week at the local pharmacy in Falher. It is extremely difficult to get a replacement. It took a lot of advertising and hoping from our local pharmacist. It turned out that Roxanne lived in Edgemont, which is the neighbouring community to my mom! Roxanne preferred to read, rather than watch TV.

## Tuesday, August 15

☻ Kalvin and Olga, a retired couple from Calgary, rang the door at 9:15 p.m. Kalvin really liked the big TV. They were on their way back home and planned to leave at 6:00 a.m. tomorrow.

## Wednesday, August 16

The weekly local newspaper had our bed and breakfast article in it! I put it up for display on my interior door, which is always covered with newspaper articles of interest, from around the area. The reporter did an excellent job!

## Thursday, August 17

☻ The cement truck came at 2:20 p.m. to pour cement in our garage. It will be neater for the kayaks and the paddle boat to rest on.

## Tuesday, August 22

☻ Sonja from Washington USA, phoned at 2:00 p.m. to reserve all three rooms at the end of September to October 8. She had been up here last year and had really liked the looks of our place, so she wrote down our number. She loved the small town, friendly people atmosphere!

## Wednesday, August 23

We got another pleasant note in the mail from Roger's former English teacher. She wanted to congratulate us on the lovely work that we had been doing to the place. When her and her husband went to Tasmania, a province in Australia, they passed through a town called Do Town, where the majority of homes had names such as Rum Do, Some Do, Do Me, Do Drop In, Do Us Too, Have To Do, Gonna Do, If I Do, and This'ill Do! Whenever she passed by our place, it reminded her of her trip!

## Friday, August 25

☻ Gretchen phoned at 7:15 p.m. to book a room for five nights, but I had to turn her down because some oil rig fellows were supposed to be with us for a month. Gretchen had read the article in the paper about us, and was looking forward to staying with us. Maybe another time!

All eight of the Tanguays arrived from Calgary for a family reunion. They let their dad/grandpa pay! Three kids went in sleeping bags. They were very polite and well-behaved! Grandpa Henri moved from McLennan in 1968 to live in Calgary. His wife, Grandma Sabrina, lived in Jean Cote. They came up here to visit their folks who live in the nursing home, a couple of times a year. Henri and Sabrina liked to stay at bed and breakfast places, especially in Quebec. Sabrina put a cooler and utensils in her van for every trip. She wasn't impressed with fast food places. She even had a tablecloth too!

## Saturday, August 26

Sabrina's grandchildren liked being able to play with all the toys and not to have to worry about not touching this or that. They brought back balloons from the reunion and then went right for the pool table!

## Sunday, August 27

Sabrina was busy making sure that everyone had eaten, as she was making buns for the trip back to Calgary. She liked to make meat pies at Christmas and took great pride in choosing which meats to buy at the specialty store. She enquired about Mannatech's weight loss products. She heard that Oprah, who was celebrating 25 years on TV, ate every three hours like the French do, to remain slim. The Tanguays were all gone by 9:00 a.m. They told others in the community how much they enjoyed it here. They were glad that they had booked us up over a month and a half ago through an e-mail.

☻ Miranda rang the doorbell at 4:50 p.m. She drove all the way from Gander Newfoundland, to be the new French and Drama teacher at the high school in town. She was very confident about her being able to get any job that she wanted, and not shy about quitting a job if it didn't suit her fancy. Being able to speak French and through her connections, she was able to be offered jobs without even showing a resumé. She was a little nervous about teaching advanced French. Being a Sunday, Miranda enquired as to which stores were open. In Nova Scotia, they were not in favour of having stores open on a Sunday. If they were, they could only sell the basic necessities like produce and bakery items. The hardware section had to be closed. Miranda will pay us on Wednesday when she gets back from her school sessions in High Prairie.

## Monday, August 28

The local hardware store in McLennan delivered our garden doors. They weighed about 400 pounds each. It will take quite a few strong fellows to lift them up, but they sure will look great!

## Tuesday, August 29

The oil rig fellows did not show, nor did they phone with any message. Gretchen and her family could have stayed with us after all. As my grandmother says who is 94 years old, people should follow the three Cs of: courage, common sense, and courtesy.

## Wednesday, August 30

☻ True to her word, Miranda came at 4:35 p.m., with her newly found teacher friend Sasha. Sasha attempted to help my daughter Leslie, play her brand new flute. Leslie was thrilled to be able to produce a note!

## Thursday, August 31

Jessenia and Jennylee drove up as we were going for a paddle boat ride. They quickly donned a lifejacket and had a ride with us. Jennylee had a turn in the single kayak to get a closer view of the duck family. Jessenia won the game of bocce that we played on the grass. Jessenia flew from the Philippines on June 26, to be with her recently married husband Riley. Riley was working on the oilrigs near Grande Prairie, so the ladies were sightseeing around northern Alberta. Jessenia teaches about 40 grade ones in the Philippines. She tries to reason with her students and says, "Very good," when they get the drift of her message. English is taught in the morning. School starts at 7:15 a.m. and finishes at 4:30 p.m. She has to clean her own classroom, there is only one old computer in the office, and there are no water heaters or class limits.

# September

## Thursday, September 14

☺ Our doorbell rang at 5:10 p.m. It had been two weeks since anyone had stayed with us. Claude was smiling at me and speaking in French. He and his wife Pauline had driven all the way from Jasper, where there were four inches of snow this morning. They needed a place to stay for tonight. They had come to see their daughter who had gotten a job at the French school in Falher. They went for dinner then returned an hour and a half later. They had a tour of the place and heard all about the improvements that we had done. Pauline's eyes were as big as saucers when she went into the cat room and saw how big our cats were. Her little cat would be a dwarf beside one of ours! Claude said that we would be busy all of the time if we were in Grande Prairie. They were in their room by 8:00 p.m.

☺ The doorbell rang again at 7:30 p.m. Two fellows working for a Quebec construction company came to spend the night. They had phoned before 6:00 p.m. to make a reservation. They had to head off to a meeting before coming here. They were excited to be in the biggest B&B in the Peace Country! Jordan and Stephan both needed to use the internet. Jordan helped Stephan with the steps needed to install the Telus kit

91

onto his laptop. Jordan phoned a business partner working in Japan. They both worked all night on their computers. They might come back on Monday. Stephan inquired what our rates would be if a construction crew came for a month. Right now they were buying land from farmers for the towns. Their last stop was in Cold Lake. Jordan left some money to cover the phone bill expenses.

## Friday, September 15

John, a single guy, drove up in his Venture van while we were working in our garage. After checking out the place, he came back an hour later and started unloading his van. John was modest, observant, and very knowledgeable about any topic. He said that everyone had some kind of a purpose in life, and it was that purpose which drove us. The more positive things a person can do, the better off people and the environment are. John was one of the first people to get a minor in environmental engineering in the 1980s. He was one of the people involved in getting Guelph, Ontario to start using the blue recycling boxes. He thought that Roger was the entertainer, whereas my daughter was the mysterious one who had made herself a cave by the dance floor. I was the tinkerer. He left us with this mathematical problem:

1) Pick a number.

2) Multiply your number by 3.

3) Add 9 to your result.

4) Divide by 3.

5) Subtract 2.

6) Subtract your original number.

7) Your answer is 1!

## *Monday, September 18*

☻ The phone rang at 8:45 p.m. It was Lydia from Falher, phoning to see if we were wheelchair accessible and if we had any room for tonight for friends of theirs. Lydia's husband was the man in charge of all the renovations that we did here, when we first bought this place. Maybelline and her French-speaking husband Jean, came over an hour later. They were from Fort St. John, which is three hours to the west of us. Jean was from Falher, but left in the 1960s to work in the oil industry. They were going to go to a morning funeral in Falher. Maybelline didn't know how she was going to get up the 13 steps in her wheelchair. She lost part of her leg to gangrene after getting a diabetic ulcer on her leg. Things were certainly different being in a wheelchair. They were surprised that all of Donnelly Corner had been wiped out. Houses that were $70 000 in Fort St. John are now $180 000. Maybelline thought that people there were very greedy for money. There was lots of that around too, with all the construction the oil boom is creating. Gasoline prices are now $1.11 there compared to $0.98 here. Jean had to climb in through the back of his truck window to get the keys that he had left in the ignition. It was a good thing that he was nimble!

☺

# Wednesday, September 20

☻The phone rang at 4:00 p.m. It was Colleen from Edmonton, inquiring about our place for a woman's hockey team. The tournament is in November, but she heard that it was hard getting rooms in the area, so she wanted to book rooms now. She phoned back at 8:00 p.m. saying that $20 a person was too much, so they would be going to a hotel.

☻Terrell rang the doorbell at 4:30 p.m. He was very pleased with the place, especially the big screen TV to watch his baseball game while he worked! Not having high speed internet didn't seem to bother him. He went to get some cash at the ATM in Falher, and to get some dinner before coming back at 6:00 p.m. He enthusiastically told me about the steel homes that he sells. They are ten times better than other homes. The technology comes from Germany. In Germany they like to shop everyday for their food, so that it is always fresh. Most work until 7:00 p.m., so they have late dinners. They don't like preservatives in their food, and are conscious of the environment. Terrell used his calling card to phone his wife. He was busy on the phone all evening; phoning clients and business partners.

# Saturday, September 23

Leigha phoned at 4:30 p.m. She was getting her modular home built and needed a place to stay until it was completed. She is having it moved to McLennan where she intends to work at the hospital. She was phoning around to get rates.

She was quite intrigued about our place and will stop by and look at it sometime.

Jessica phoned me at 10:00 p.m., apologizing for phoning so late. She had e-mailed me yesterday and needed to confirm a room for two nights this week. I usually don't go to bed until past midnight, so it was no problem. She will be in the bunk bed room since the other two rooms are already booked up. I had just come across one of Jessica's notes from a previous visit this morning, as I was cleaning up my office. She had jotted down that she was off for a run and to thank me for the stay. It was quite the coincidence that she phoned today!

## Sunday, September 24

☻ Leigha and her friend came for a tour. She loved it the moment she set her eyes on it. Compared to other places that she asked about, our $315 a week was cheap. The other place that she went to wanted $500 or more for a week. She tried out the new elliptical machine and took a business card. She liked the sound of running water from our fountain. She was from British Columbia and could easily fall asleep to the sound of any water.

☻ Colleen phoned me back at 7:00 p.m. She had succeeded in getting a motel room for most of her hockey team, except for her family! She booked up the double room for two nights in November. If we had more rooms, she would have placed others with us too.

☺

# Monday, September 25

☻ Pete walked in the door at 5:55 p.m. We were just arriving ourselves. He was the low man on the totem pole, with the water canal project. His job was to survey the land from Winagami to Girouxville. He came from Edmonton and was recommended to stay at Itlldo Place by others in his company, who had come over the summer. He was related by marriage to Sally. Sally was one of the local bus drivers who fifteen years ago was my school aide. It was amazing how we are all connected somehow! Pete went to get take-out at the local confectionary store. He enjoyed watching the Edmonton Oilers play.

# Tuesday, September 26

☻ Sonja and Nanton arrived at 6:20 p.m., to drop off their refrigerated trailer that they will put the geese and ducks in. Sonja is here until Friday to take pictures of the hunters in action, as well as the wildlife. She missed taking a good picture of a bull-moose eating in the marsh, because she had left her good camera in Seattle. Her husband and his friends will come on Saturday. Sonja was going to bring us smoked salmon, but because of the border patrol workers going on strike, she thought that it would be best not to instigate trouble. They had two girls at home, an 8 and 10 year old. They were married one year after us. Nanton liked hunting up here, because the geese aren't educated yet on the dangers of hunters. There are also lots to hunt! Sonja said that in Washington, the Gala apples are pronounced with a long a vowel for the first a! Nanton is sure that they will have a great time.

☻ Jessica arrived at 10:00 p.m. The door was unlocked for her to come in. She had just driven five hours from Edmonton non-stop. She enjoyed seeing the indoor fountain and elliptical machine improvements. Being tired, she didn't realize that the ladder to climb up to the top bunk was by the wardrobe. She climbed up at the end of the bed so that she could read her book in the better light!

## *Wednesday, September 27*

☺ Jessica left at 6:30 a.m. to go to her breakfast date in Peace River at Smitty's. The fellow that she was meeting was heading to Falher. There was no place in Falher open that early for breakfast, so they decided to meet in Peace River. There was lots of fog too. Jessica had lunch with two principals. Lots of eating out! Tomorrow she will go to the French immersion school in Falher, to do more speech therapy. The principal there wanted a business card from us, so that she too could send us people, who needed to do some business at her school. Jessica said that Edmonton was experiencing a great population increase. There was lots of work to do there. Roger and I put a table in her room so that she could work in private. She was pretty tired with all of the traveling and getting up early.

☺

# Thursday, September 28

☺Jessica left at 8:30 a.m. to see students for speech therapy. Pete went to see Sally tonight. With only 300 people living in Donnelly, it wasn't hard to find her house. Sonja bought a Cute-as-Can-Bee insect cage off of Leslie for $3.50. Her husband will bring it back for her, since she was flying back home to be with their kids and didn't have lots of room in her luggage. Sonja and Nanton went visiting too. On their last trip up here in October 2005, they became friends with Roger's aunt and uncle who lived across the road from us. They had a nice visit.

# Friday, September 29

Sonja and Nanton left early this morning, keeping up their typical routine. She will be able to show her family and friends in Washington, her Canadian wildlife pictures! The plane that Sonja will take is the plane that Kolton and Hank are going to be arriving on. They are hunting buddies of Nanton's. The guys will have a night out in Grande Prairie, before coming back here tomorrow.

# Saturday, September 30

Kolton worked with Nanton. They go around the world buying pieces of equipment. They used to come to Canada a lot, but now that the Canadian dollar is about the same value as the American dollar, they are choosing to shop elsewhere.

Hank was a cook who had his own business. He was going to cook up a goose on the grill, but decided not to.

# October

## Tuesday, October 3

Nanton and Kolton drove Hank back to Grande Prairie. He could only get a few days off of work to go hunting. Nanton was getting to be an expert at driving back and forth from Grande Prairie! They liked to stay out late and go to the bars.

## Thursday, October 5

Nanton got a call about some equipment that he needed. He and Kolton had to take off immediately to drive back home, then on to the Panama Canal of all places, to make the deal. Talk about a lot of traveling! Nanton paid in American and Canadian dollars. He packed up his pillows and blanket that he had brought.

☺ Alvin phoned at 4:30 p.m. to see if we had room for him and his working buddies. They were working at the local arena, fixing up the heating and cooling systems. I did not know at the time that the Americans were not coming back tonight, as they had said their good-byes to Roger while I was at work, so I told Alvin that we only had room for him.

After contacting Roger to see if the Americans were gone, I left a voice message for Alvin that we would have room for all of them. He unfortunately didn't check his messages. His buddies slept in Falher, and he arrived at 10:00 p.m. Alvin will be back on the 18th to finish up his job. He will pay us for both nights then. He said that he was very honest. Alvin lived in Stettler.

## Saturday, October 7

☻ The doorbell rang at 9:05 p.m. It was Henry and Rebecca. Their three year old son was tired and their baby daughter was already sleeping. They needed a place for the night after having driven four and a half hours from Drayton Valley. Rebecca's mom was sick in McLennan's hospital. They settled their kids in, before watching TV for the night.

## Sunday, October 8

Rebecca and Henry played games with their kids. Tyler, the three year old took a felt and scribbled all over the painting easel. There were toys all over the place when they left.

☻ Margo rang the doorbell at 9:35 p.m. She was a divorced nurse who was trying her luck out at being a medic on the oilrigs. She wasn't feeling very good, so she declined our offer to go out and have some hotdogs and marshmallows over the firepit. She lived in Grande Prairie.

☺

## Friday, October 13

☺ The doorbell rang at 4:30 p.m. It was a former classmate of Roger's, whose 93 year old mother had just passed away in McLennan. Justin and his wife owned their own trucking business in Fort St. John. Their 20 year old son, who was a chef at the well-known Egan's restaurant, and their younger son Alexander, also stayed for one night. Justin left the Smoky River area when he was 19 years old, to go work at the pulp mill in Grande Prairie. He was happy to be back in the area.

We got a reservation for Saturday, November 11. There is a big birthday going on.

## Tuesday, October 17

☺ True to his word, Alvin rang the doorbell at 4:40 p.m. He was anxious to watch TV, then to get a bite to eat at the local confectionary. He had been working at the arena again. The special unit that was installed, monitors interior temperature and lighting. At 9:00 p.m. the TV went off and he went in his room to read up on tomorrow's work. He didn't bother to close the blinds before going to bed, since it was dark at night and in the morning now.

## Thursday, October 19

☺ The doorbell rang at 7:10 p.m. It was Harold who had to use the washroom and wanted to know where to get a bite to eat in the area. He saw the construction that we were doing to replace the garden doors with energy efficient ones.

## Sunday, October 22

☻ The phone rang at 8:00 p.m. It was Karen from British Columbia, phoning to enquire if we had any rooms available for tomorrow. She phoned back at 8:05 p.m. to see if we took cards for payment or if we would prefer cash or cheque. She will be coming between eight and nine o'clock.

## Monday, October 23

☻ Sure enough, Karen arrived at 8:35 p.m. She had taken an hour for supper in Falher and unbeknownst to her, this fellow from New Brunswick who had driven five days to Alberta for work, was checking her out. He came with a younger fellow to our B&B to check it out. $315 a week was too much for him to pay. He preferred to speak French. With a shake of Karen's hand, he was off. Karen travels about to different doctors, to educate them about new practices. Her last time up here was two years ago. To get back to Vancouver, she has to travel to Peace River, fly to Calgary, then on to Vancouver by the early afternoon.

☻ The doorbell rang at 9:45 p.m. It was a kindly looking gentleman, who apologized for ringing the door so late. Lawrence was on his way to Slave Lake to supervise home-schooling children. He had a reservation in a motel in Valleyview, but decided to stay with us instead, since it would gain him an hour and a half traveling time. He was also already tired. He has to be off by six in the morning. He phoned to cancel his reservation and to talk to his wife in Edson. She phoned him back so that he wouldn't have to use up his calling card. He admired my baby grand as he was talking to his family. One of his sons was teaching piano and was attempting to teach him how to play as well. It was hard to squeeze in a half an hour of practicing a day!

## Tuesday, October 24

Marion phoned from New Brunswick, to make a reservation for her boyfriend on November 11 and 12. We are already booked up for the 11th, so he will come for the 12th.

## Sunday, October 29

☻ The phone rang at 6:10 p.m. It was Serge phoning about the big birthday during the November 11th weekend. He has family from out of town that needs a place to stay. We are booked up for most of that weekend already.

## Tuesday, October 31

We had twice as many trick-or-treaters this year compared to last year. They came to check out the bed and breakfast and to go through our haunted maze that Leslie had created on the dance floor. The kids were thrilled with it! The more wooden dolls that they found, the more candy Leslie gave them!

# November

## Saturday, November 4

☻ Marion's boyfriend phoned at 7:00 p.m. to cancel his reservation for the 100th birthday coming up. He hoped that he was giving us enough time to re-book the room.

## Sunday, November 5

I got an e-mail from a group that was looking for accommodations for some youths who would like to volunteer in our area. They would be here until August.

☻ William popped in at 4:40 p.m. to let us know that his wife and four young children, as well as another couple would be coming tomorrow and leaving on Friday. He was a framer and was finishing up work on a shed. His wife Julia, taught their ten year old boy Jeffery through home-schooling, because of the constant traveling about. His sisters were too young yet.

☺

# Monday, November 6

The group organizer e-mailed me back saying that she was able to locate a rental house for the youths in Girouxville.

☻ William and his family, as well as Susan and Gerald came at 1:30 p.m. The kids were full of energy exploring the place and playing with the toys! They had lots of laughs watching Mr. Bean on video. It was the show where Mr. Bean was trying to eat a candy in church and not wanting to be caught in the action! At midnight, the smoke detector in the bunk bed room where the children slept went off. It was a beep now and then to announce that the battery was low. The children never even heard it.

# Tuesday, November 7

☻ The phone rang at 6:15 p.m. It was Kristen from Calgary, getting some information on our bed and breakfast for five guys who would be working at the local high school for a week, doing a residency program. The fellows wanted to know the rates, if we had a TV and internet access, what was for breakfast, and if any cats were allowed access to the rooms. Kristen will let us know tomorrow.

William ended up with soaking boots from all the snow at work. Roger leaned them up and put a heater to them. It took four hours to dry them out! William's two year old daughter was sick and crying during the night. They went to bed at 10:30 p.m. William was off by seven in the morning.

# Wednesday, November 8

☻ Sure enough at 7:10 p.m., Kristen phoned back to say that the fellows would be staying with us on Sunday through to Friday morning.

Susan was home by herself watching TV and doing needle point. She was working on a fall forest scene. It was amazing to see all the counting and tracking of colours that she had to do. One of the tropical fish was doing a somersault dance. I scooped it out so that the four year old girl wouldn't be upset seeing a dead fish in the morning. It was Susan's birthday today! Leslie gave her a birthday card that she had made.

# Thursday, November 9

Susan was busy cooking hamburgers on the griddle for everyone. She ran out of sugar, so I filled up the container for her. They wanted to use clean towels everyday, so the laundry had to be done also.

☻ Birgit phoned at 5:45 p.m. to see if we had rooms available for Friday and Saturday. Her friends were expecting to stay at her place for the 100th birthday party, but she was already full. We too are full for Saturday.

# Friday, November 10

☻ William and his family left at 4:30 p.m. William learned to speak English 14 years ago. They speak high and low German, some Spanish and of course English. William felt that it was very important to know different languages. He couldn't understand people who move to another country, yet don't feel that they have to learn the language of the country. I gave him a book to give to his children about a kitten. They are headed off to La Crete which is four hours north of Donnelly. They are back in the area on Tuesday. Unfortunately we are already booked up for the week. William said that he wished that he had known about us sooner. Having four kids in a hotel room was like prison. He gave us a $75 bonus!

## Saturday, November 11

All the final touches are done in the bathrooms. The new paneling looks great, as well as the new baseboards.

It was a good thing that Patricia had reserved tonight way back on October 13. It turned out that it was the 25th reunion at the local high school and a 100th birthday celebration. Patricia phoned us just as her vehicle was entering Donnelly. She wasn't sure if she had the right place or not. She thought that our place was blue when in fact it was brown. She and her husband popped in at 3:55 p.m., to take a quick peek before heading to the birthday. Patricia was sure that her granddaughter would like riding on Leslie's rocking horse and playing ball. Her daughter and son-in-law also stayed for the night.

Roger got another booking at the clothing shop in Falher. It was for her husband's birthday in December. She wants to surprise him!

☻ The doorbell rang at 5:35 p.m. It was Jean-Luc from Peace River, with his wife. Jean-Luc went to the same school as Roger, so they got caught up with some news. Jean-Luc had been at our place when it was a bar and restaurant. He was interested in seeing all of the changes that we had done. They didn't come back till after midnight.

## Sunday, November 12

Hugo was simply delighted to show his daughter around our place this morning. He couldn't believe all the stuff that there was to do! Hugo does carpentry work in Dawson Creek. His wife enjoyed playing hockey and looking after their daughter Kiasha. Patricia had a good time visiting with everyone at the birthday party. They left at 10:45 a.m.

☺ Jean-Luc and his wife got up at 11:00 a.m. While Sharon was in the shower, Roger played some tunes on the piano and keyboard for Jean-Luc. Jean-Luc was in the paper mill industry for over 20 years, now he is in the oil industry. They left at 11:25 a.m.

☻ The phone rang at 4:05 p.m. It was Mary calling from Edmonton to say that they would be arriving around 10:00 p.m. tonight. They actually showed up at 10:50 p.m. There was fog in the air as the temperature rose three degrees to minus ten! There were two ladies and three men from Quest Theatre in Calgary. Two of them recently graduated from the same high school as I did. Neat! Made me feel old though! They were quite impressed with the fitness section and the musical instruments that they could use.

# Monday, November 13

I brought down the dial-up starter package for Jason's computer. He'll set it up later tonight. They had to be at the school by 8:00 a.m. They arrived back at 5:55 p.m. Mary tried the elliptical machine, but it was squeaking so she stopped. Roger went to fix it. Another problem was that they couldn't get the volume to work on the TV. It was just on the wrong channel. Throughout the evening, some were practicing play fighting on the dance floor, exercising on the bicycle, playing on the keyboard, watching TV, eating popcorn, discussing lines, and generally visiting.

# Tuesday, November 14

☻ Our guests didn't arrive until 9:15 p.m. They had supper in Peace River for a change.

☻ The phone rang at 3:30 p.m. It was Sheila seeing if we had a room available for the Friday and Saturday tournament coming up. She wanted to bring her boyfriend. The rest of her team was camping out in the school's gym. We were all booked up.

# Wednesday, November 15

Everyone had about 90 students in their group. Practically the whole school was involved in the Quest Theatre production that would take place on Friday. Lots of work to do yet!

## Thursday, November 16

Things were falling into place. It should be okay for tomorrow's production!

## Friday, November 17

☺ The theatrical group was up, packed and gone by 8:10 a.m. They were a great bunch of young people!

The woman's hockey team from B.C. came after their game around 11:00 p.m. The two ten year olds and the two year old were happy to go to sleep. Seven women played on the team and two guys came as well. Five camped out on the dance floor.

## Saturday, November 18

● The only hockey game that was played today was at 5:00 p.m. in McLennan. They played with our board games. Their favorite was Cranium. The group wasn't interested in going to the dance. Everyone was asleep before 11:00 p.m.

## Sunday, November 19

☺ The woman had a game at 9:00 a.m. As soon as the game was over, they packed up and were gone within 15 minutes. They were anxious to get back home to their families in Taylor. They had a good time and will probably come back in February for Roger's hockey tournament, if he can find three more women's teams.

## Saturday, November 25

☻ Tony phoned at 3:00 p.m. to inquire about rooms for a crew that would be working in McLennan on the new senior's facility. There would be eight men. Tony will come tomorrow to take a look.

## Sunday, November 26

Tony was ringing the doorbell which was frozen with the minus 33 weather. He ended up knocking which got my attention! He thought that the room was more than enough space for the older men on the crew. He made up a code for the door just in case they arrive tomorrow. They will probably come on Wednesday when it warms up a bit.

## Monday, November 27

☻ Tony phoned at 7:00 p.m., to say that the men wouldn't be arriving until later on in the week.

## Tuesday, November 28

☻ The phone rang at 4:00 p.m. Three couples and their children might be coming in the middle of February for a wedding. Edith, who is a nurse in McLennan, will come sometime to check it out.

## *Wednesday, November 29*

The principal who came in April, e-mailed me about the sign that he wants to put up on our property, to promote his school. It will have to wait now until the spring, because of all the snow and cold weather.

# December

## Monday, December 4

☺ The phone rang at 9:50 a.m. It was Cecilia from the local French radio station. She was wondering if we would want to sponsor some 15 seconds of thank you ads, for the volunteer youths who were in the community for three months. Roger will go tomorrow to help create the ad for our bed and breakfast.

● The phone rang at 3:40 p.m. It was Tony seeing if we still had openings for two of his fellows. Vance and Scott showed up a half an hour later. They headed out to Falher for supper and to get some groceries. They were helping to put up the steel frames for the senior's facility. If they have time, they will help to put up the walls too. Being single, they didn't mind coming here from Edmonton, to be paid the big bucks for ten days! It didn't take them long to settle in and to watch a hockey game with Roger.

## Tuesday, December 5

Roger went to the radio station to listen to the ad. He asked them to put Christmas sounding music to it, and to put

Itlldo Place Bed and Breakfast instead of just Itlldo Bed and Breakfast. It will be aired twice at day, for a total of 25 times.

☺ Vance and Scott were at work at 7:00 a.m. They came back for lunch at 1:45 p.m., then back again for the evening at 6:10 p.m. They had a great day, although they were dripping sweat with warmth from where they were working. The warmest place was on the top floor. Most of the time they were wearing t-shirts like it was in Hawaii! They cooked a pizza for supper and watched TV.

## Wednesday, December 6

Vance and Scott left a little later today because of a region-wide power outage. It was nice to sleep in a bit! They made $20 and hour and after eight hours of work, it rose to $30 an hour. They also got $100 living allowance each day. Scott's girlfriend from Ontario will be coming for six days. Everyone will leave on December 22. Vance liked petting our dogs. He thought that they were really friendly. He cooked fish on the grill for supper.

## Thursday, December 7

Both Vance and Scott had sore backs from lifting heavy equipment today. They were sprawled out on the couches watching TV.

☺

## Friday, December 8

The main course for supper that they tucked into was pork chops, and then they finished up their fourth box of beer. They went outside into their car to smoke, while listening to their tunes.

## Saturday, December 9

Vance and Scott liked coming back here for their lunch. They got an hour and a half for lunch, minus thirty minutes travelling. They listened to the music channel on the TV, while they munched down their lunch. I let both of them know that tomorrow would be housework day and that I would be going into their rooms to clean. Vance offered to strip his bed for me.

## Sunday, December 10

Both Vance and Scott were tired tonight. I showed them the baby guppy that was born this week. Vance had figured that the mom was pregnant. She was so full looking. I put a glass in the bathroom by each sink. It was a tip I read about on a bed and breakfast site.

## Monday, December 11

Vance and Scott are going to be leaving on Friday and coming back on Sunday with their girlfriends for another week.

☺ Simon phoned at 9:10 a.m. to see if we had any rooms available. His mother-in-law passed away yesterday. Since most of his family members are old, they decided that the bunk bed room wouldn't be possible. He will keep us in mind for another time.

## Tuesday, December 12

● William phoned at 12:50pm. He was one of the builders who stayed at our place with the four children. They were going to be in the area for a bit and wanted to know if we had room for them. Unfortunately we did not.

## Wednesday, December 13

☺ Pat phoned at 10:55am. She was enquiring about a midget hockey team staying here at the end of January. She'll get back to us.

Vance and Scott made some phone calls tonight to get ready for their Friday arrivals. Roger clarified with them that they were responsible for cleaning up their own dishes.

## Thursday, December 14

Roger went to McLennan where Vance and Scott work, to ask Tony about how we were going to be paid. All we had to do was to fax in the bill to their Edmonton office. Roger spent a half an hour chatting with Tony. He was quite the young fellow to be overseeing such an operation. He needed people to work on steel studs like on the exterior wall, interior wall, bulkhead/ suspension, frames, panel installation, joists, Comflor/decking. Then there was the insulation for the exterior and interior wall, plus a vapour barrier. Drywall was next for the exterior, walls, ceiling, patching, taping, corner bead/trims, and sanding. For the acoustic ceiling, there was the wire, t-bar, mould and tiles. The stucco had a lot with vapour/air barriers, foam insulation base coat/ mesh, finishing coat, flashings, and specialty stucco. The demountable partitions had steel framing, vinyl boards, trims, frames, insulation and baffles. For the miscellaneous tasks, there was: delivery, clean-up, demolition, traveling, scaffolding/hoisting, caulking and anything else that hadn't been thought of. Tony will keep us in mind if more workers need a place to stay after Christmas.

The fellows stayed up a bit longer tonight, since they were not going to go to work tomorrow.

## Friday, December 15

Vance and Scott were up bright and early anyway. It's hard to readjust your internal sleeping pattern. They called Roger down before heading out to Edmonton, to say their goodbyes. They were going to be leaving their work equipment and boots here. They will come back on Sunday night around 6:00 p.m., for their last week here.

☻ The phone rang at 1:10 p.m. It was Nikki from the Peace River Tourism Association, wishing to book up a room for the Smoky River Trade Show in March. Boy is she ever early!

☻ The phone rang again at 8:00 p.m. It was Nellie, wanting to book a room for three nights at the end of December. Her sister from Quebec stayed with us this year, and highly recommended us. We could help her out for two of the nights. She will phone us back with her final decision in a couple of days.

## Sunday, December 17

☻ Scott and Charla arrived at 5:40 p.m. They went to their bedroom after a tour of the place. Vance arrived at 7:55 p.m. He got a ride with another fellow from Edmonton. He and Roger chatted and watched TV for awhile.

## Monday, December 18

Charla spent part of the day here. She was from Ontario and was studying early childhood education. She was particularly interested in working with special needs children. One little boy that she was working with was the poster boy for a hospital. She was so pleased that he could say her name. Some children need braces, others communicate through sign language and special devices. She was glad to be spending some time with Scott.

## Tuesday, December 19

Charla got up around noon. She enjoyed being able to have a sleep in! The baby guppy fish that was born last week was going to be named after her, but it died because of the water change. The change of water was too much for her. She was barely over one centimeter.

Roger was able to get in contact with Nikki about the trade show reservation. She was glad to know that we still had openings.

## Wednesday, December 20

When we got home from the school's Christmas concert, Vance was fast asleep on the couch, with the TV still on. He must have worked over-time.

The principal at the elementary school in Falher might have a teacher wanting to stay at our place for a month in January, until she can find a place of her own. It will be up to her.

☻ The phone rang at 9:25 p.m. It was Nellie phoning to say that she was able to find a motel that had a cancellation, so she will be staying there for the three days of her holiday.

## Thursday, December 21

The guests didn't have to work tomorrow, so they were celebrating with loud music and drinks. Scott might be coming back after Christmas. All of them really enjoyed staying here. I left a Christmas gift by the door for them.

☺

# Friday, December 22

Scott drove Vance to High Prairie, so that he could get a ride to Edmonton. When Scott came back to pick up his girlfriend, his transmission in his car gave out. He had to get it towed to High Prairie, and his dad kindly drove all the way from Edmonton to pick them up. By the time his dad used the washroom and they had a chat, they cautiously left at 4:30 p.m., with Leslie waving good-bye from the lighted hallway upstairs.

They were our last guests of the year! I was wondering who might be coming in through our doors this year, and now I have plenty of memories and names in my guest book from those willing enough to sign in. Running a bed and breakfast has been mostly an enjoyable experience! I am eager to see who might be staying with us in the year coming up! There are hockey tournaments, trade shows, weddings, funerals, vacationers, and working people. The world is a small place, and you never know when our paths might cross. As the radio station said for us, "Best wishes for the coming year, from Itlldo Place Bed and Breakfast, Donnelly."

Check out the places where our guests have been from, perhaps your town or city will be added to our growing list!

**Alberta**: Airdrie, Ardrossan, Athabaska, Barrhead, Beaverlodge, Berwyn, Bonnyville, Boyle, Brooks, Calgary, Camrose, Cardston, Didsbury, Dixonville, Donnelly, Drayton Valley, Eaglesham, Edmonton, Enilda, Fairview, Falher, Fawcett, Fort McMurray, Gibbons, Girouxville, Grande Cache, Grande Prairie, Grimshaw, Guy, High Level, High Prairie, Hussar, Innisfail, Lac La Biche, Lacombe,

Leduc, Legal, Lethbridge, Lloydminster, Manning, Marie-Reine, Mayorthorpe, McLennan, Meander River, Morinville, Nampa, Nanton, New Fish Creek, Okotoks, Olds, Peace River, Ponoka, Priddis, Red Deer, Rocky Mountain House, St. Albert, St. Isidore, Sexsmith, Sherwood Park, Silver Valley, Slave Lake, Spirit River, Standard, Stavely, Stettler, Stony Plain, Sundre, Thorsby, Valleyview, Wainwright, Warburg, Watino, Wembley, Westlock, Whitecourt, Whitemud, and Willingdon.

**British Columbia**: Blind Bay, Crawford Bay, Dawson Creek, Farmington, Fort St. John, Kamloops, Kelowna, Mackenzie, Mission, Nanaimo, Parksville, Penticton, Pouce Coupe, Powell River, Prince George, Sayward, Taylor, Vancouver, Vanderhoof, Vernon, and Victoria.

**Manitoba**: Grunthal.

**Newfoundland & Labrador**: Eastport and Gander.

**Northwest Territories**: Hay River and Yellowknife.

**Ontario**: Hamilton, Niagara Falls and Ottawa.

**Prince Edward Island**: Little Pond.

**Quebec**: Chicoutimi, Montreal, Quebec City, Rimouski, St. Ephrem, and Terrebonne.

**Saskatchewan**: Archerville, Bellevue, Carrot River, Jackfish Lake, Livelong, Meadow Lake, Melfort, Moose Jaw, Okla, Prince Albert, St. Denis, St. Louis, Saskatoon, Shaunavon, Swift Current and Tisdale.

**Yukon**: Whitehorse.

# International

**Alaska**: Anchorage.

**Cyprus**: Limassal.

**Florida**: Pensacola.

**France**: Marseille and Paris.

**Germany**: Breslauer and Weisbaden.

**Idaho**: Boise, Idaho Falls and Rigby.

**Illinois**: Chicago and Kankakee.

**Japan**: Higasi, Sinagawa and Tokyo.

**New Jersey**: Monroe Township.

**New Mexico**: Farmington.

**North Dakota**: Wildrose.

**Ohio**: Cleveland.

**Philippines**: Mangaldan.

**Washington**: Buckley, Hobart and Seattle.

Itlldo Place Bed and Breakfast will be up for sale in the year 2013! Our 3.5 acres is located on highway #2, at the entrance to the Village of Donnelly. We are 425 km northwest of Edmonton, Alberta, Canada, at GPS location:

N 55°43.453˙
W 117° 06.363˙

☺ For inquiries, to offer us a bid, or to make a reservation, you can contact Dana Wood-Boissonneault or Roger Boissonneault at itlldo@telusplanet.net or 1-780-925-2376.

The dugout stocked with Grass Carp.

Three-door garage with plenty of room!

Establishment plaque stating when the first guests arrived.

Welcome to the Double Room!

Sun streaming into the Queen Room.

Bunk beds for children or grown-ups.

Movies anyone? The pull-out bed will get you really close!

Care for some food or drinks?

The kitchenette has lots of appliances.

Four sinks, two toilets and one shower are in the woman's
bathroom, which is wheelchair accessible.

Two-level stage with a grand piano on the dance floor.

Quality Usborne books for sale.

Four wall fountains with plants and lights.

Convenient gym and exercise balls.

Elliptical machine, bicycle, rowing machine, abs builder, and min-trampoline.

Sport stacking the 3-6-3 and the Cycle.

Roger and Leslie playing foosball at the 4-in-1, with air
hockey, hockey, and pool a flip away.

Paddle boat, double kayak and single kayak.

Mini-basketball court.

Itlldo Creek running in the spring.

Two-level deck with a walk-out patio.

Two herons in the raised flower garden.

Sundial garden with the dry creek and bridge,
leading into the dugout.

A comfortable spot to enjoy the outside.

The perfect hammock to get away from it all!

Benches to view the muskrats, fish, ducks, and birds from.

Two birdhouses and a feeder.

The second creek that helps to fill
the dugout up with water.

A campfire for those long summer days.

One of the many gorgeous sunsets.